2- 15-90

# WHY YOUR CHILD IS HYPERACTIVE

# WHY YOUR CHILD IS HYPERACTIVE

## Ben F. Feingold, M.D.

Random House New York

Library of Congress Cataloging in Publication Data
Feingold, Ben F
    Why your child is hyperactive.
    1. Hyperkinesia.  2.  Food additives—Toxicology.
I.  Title.  [DNLM:  1.  Diet therapy—Popular works.
2.  Hyperkinesis—Popular works.  WS350 F299w]
RJ506.H9F44          618.9′28′5          74-9078
ISBN 0-394-49343-5

Manufactured in the United States of America
2468B9753

To my wife,
Helene Samuels Feingold,
initial supporter of my thesis

# Author's Note

This book was made possible through the interest and support of many individuals to whom I am indebted. Until my own experiences were duplicated by other scientists, encouragement and confidence was extremely important in the early developmental period of the San Francisco Kaiser-Permanente Diet.

I wish to thank Dr. David Boesel, of the National Institute of Education, Department of Health, Education and Welfare, for his early appreciation of my observations. This led to the application of my hypothesis in a study at the Human Resources Institute of Boston University, funded by the N.I.E.

Dr. Wilson Riles, California State Superintendent of Schools, has earned my deep gratitude for his early adoption of the program for a study in the Santa Cruz school system under the direction of Drs. David Sweet and Lawrence Ernst, Superintendent of Elementary Schools.

For support of my studies I wish to thank Dr. Clifford Keene, president of the Kaiser Foundation Hospitals; Dr. Cecil Cutting, Medical Director, and Dr. John G. Smillie, Assistant Director of the Kaiser-Permanente Group.

For administrative assistance I thank Mr. Robert Jack and Mrs. Ivanelle Childers, of the Kaiser Research Institute; for early assistance in developing a clinical and research program, my appreciation goes to Drs. J. Hicks Williams, John Mann and Anthony J. Nespole, of the Santa Clara, California, Kaiser-Permanente Medical Center.

I express my appreciation and admiration to Judith Keithley for her successful development of pilot programs at the schools in South San Francisco and San Mateo, California.

I am indebted to my aide, Mary Ann Warr Giacona, who never failed to perform in the presence of many pressures.

Finally, I am particularly grateful to the many individuals from all walks of life—especially those troubled and harassed parents and grandparents who wrote and phoned me. They provided a broad perspective of the problem.

San Francisco, Calif.                    Ben F. Feingold, M.D.
March 1, 1974

# Contents

| | Author's Note | vii |
|---|---|---|
| 1 | Behavior Is Related to Diet | I |
| 2 | The Role of Allergy | II |
| 3 | Behavior Linked to Artificial Colors and Flavors | I5 |
| 4 | Four Hyperactive Boys | 22 |
| 5 | Diet Controls Hyperactivity | 30 |
| 6 | A Mother's Diary | 44 |
| 7 | The Patterns of Hyperactivity | 49 |
| 8 | The Hazards of Treatment with Drugs | 60 |
| 9 | Success and Failure with the Diet | 68 |
| 10 | The Problem of Food Labeling | 77 |
| 11 | The Problem of Medications for Children | 92 |
| 12 | Letters from Parents | 98 |

## CONTENTS

| 13 | The Story of Food Colors | 109 |
| 14 | The Synthetic Food Flavors | 122 |
| 15 | How Safe Are "Safe Additives"? | 131 |
| 16 | Genetics and Behavior | 139 |
| 17 | The Need for Research | 148 |
| 18 | The Pollutants We Ingest | 156 |
| | The K-P Diet | 169 |
| | Sample Menus | 182 |
| | Suggested Recipes | 201 |

# WHY
# YOUR
# CHILD IS
# HYPERACTIVE

# 1

## Behavior
## Is Related to Diet

In the summer of 1965 a woman entered my office in the allergy clinic of the Kaiser-Permanente Medical Center, which sprawls over a gentle hilltop in San Francisco, California. In her early forties, she was a member of the health care program and lived in Oakland.

She was suffering from acute hives. Her face was swollen, mainly about the eyes. An eruption of the skin, giant hives can be moderately painful and unsightly to the point of the grotesque. She looked, and obviously felt, miserable.

I read the medical history of this patient, examined her and tested her for allergy. Since the tests were negative, I concluded that artificial food colors and flavors might be involved. Food additives had been a causative factor in previous cases of hives that I had seen. I immediately placed her on a diet to which she quickly responded. The skin condition vanished within seventy-two hours.

Then, some ten days following the diet prescription, I

received an unusual call from the Center's chief of psychiatry. He asked, "What did you do with that patient?" and I replied that we had simply "placed her on the elimination diet."

The psychiatrist then revealed that this woman had been in psychotherapy for about two years. She'd been hostile and aggressive, unable to get along with her husband or family or co-workers. In less than two weeks, these conditions had also cleared.

I was startled. Understandably, the patient had not volunteered the information about psychotherapy, and the psychiatric records had not accompanied her regular medical history. At Kaiser, to protect the privacy of the patient, such information is available only after special arrangements have been made with the approval of both the psychiatrist and the patient.

However, the fact remained that with diet control eliminating food colors and flavors, the giant hives had disappeared and her behavior had become quite normal. The psychiatrist, equally surprised, reported that she was now "adjusting at home and at work."

I was truly baffled and phoned the patient, requesting that she return to the clinic for conference. Soon she sat across the desk from me, skin now normal, and reported the exact findings of the psychiatrist—that her behavior had completely changed. Further, she said that any infraction of the diet brought back the full constellation of previous complaints.

While I found the case extremely interesting, I also had to consider the possibility of coincidence. Patients frequently have multiple complaints which may respond at the same time to a given treatment, and the reasons are difficult to determine. Though a medication occasionally does a dual job, no medication had been prescribed for this patient. Only diet. Perhaps there was a psychological response to the diet? I didn't know.

Since we had no previous experience or knowledge of a behavioral disturbance induced by artificial colors and flavors, I became curious and alerted the staff to look for similar situations.

Not only in medicine, but in many fields of science, one important observation can lead to another, although they do not, on the surface, appear to be related. Such was the experience that led to diet control for the Oakland woman and later brought about observations linking behavioral disturbances in some children to the food synthetics. Along the same indirect route, research completely unrelated to hyperkinesis–learning disability (H-LD) provided the San Francisco Kaiser-Permanente Diet with possible management of these troubled young people—an alternative to drugs.

Strangely enough, my observations of the adverse reactions to food additives in general, and those of the hyperkinetic child in particular, grew from studies on the allergic reaction to flea bites. The medical adventure from the lowly pest to the hyperactive child stretched over many years.

In 1951 I had given up an association in the private practice of allergy in Los Angeles to join the Kaiser Medical Care Program in Northern California as chief of the Department of Allergy. I had already practiced medicine for twenty-two years, beginning as a pediatrician, shifting slowly to specialize in child allergy, then expanding to treatment of both adult and child patients. Believing the Permanente program was a new trend in medicine, I also hoped it would give me time to do research—a lifelong personal ambition of mine.

Settling down to the new job, with headquarters at the main medical center in San Francisco, I established allergy clinics at several of the area hospitals, as well as a central laboratory for the preparation of allergens, chemical substances to be used in diagnosis and treatment.

Research phases began within a few months. I learned that the common flea was quite a problem in the sophisticated Bay region. For reasons unknown, the wingless, high-leaping insect of the order Siphonaptera has always cherished the shores and fields and hills around the Golden Gate.

Complaining bitterly and scratching vigorously, early visitors and residents encountered them in Barbary Coast saloons, in hostelries and homes, and on the rancheros. In tribute to the pest, a main thoroughfare that crosses San Mateo County from the southern border of San Francisco to Palo Alto, in Santa Clara County, is called Alameda de las Pulgas (Park of the Fleas).

With this colorful history in the background, I received a number of requests from agitated modern patients for treatment and protection against the tiny but mighty insect. We had no flea allergen, so I undertook to prepare a specific extract for diagnosis and treatment.

Since I would probably need a large number of fleas for the work, I asked the California Academy of Sciences to provide information on the whereabouts of a "round million of the pests," simply as a source of fleas for preparation of extracts. I was referred to the local Communicable Disease Center (known as the Plague Station since the 1909 bubonic outbreak in the Bay Area) of U.S. Public Health. Although unable to provide the insects, Plague Station officials immediately recognized that no one understood the nature of flea-bite reaction and suggested that I apply to the National Institutes of Health, a government agency, for a grant. Not long after, a Washington review team visited San Francisco and the grant was approved, then funded, leading to the establishment of the Laboratory of Medical Entomology, Kaiser Foundation Research Institute, of which I became director.

We launched our intriguing project. Two young entomologists, Eleazar Benjamini and Dov Michaeli, joined our staff. Very soon we developed techniques for mass rearing of various species of fleas, and before long, the Kaiser Research Institute was the proud father of a million fleas a week.

Eventually we demonstrated that the reaction to the flea bite was induced by a low (molecular weight) chemical present in the saliva of the insect. In the field of immunology (the branch of medicine which deals with immunity or protection from disease), a low-molecular-weight chemical is known as a *hapten*.

Because of its size, the little hapten is unable to induce either an immune or an allergic response. However, when combined with proteins, which are larger-molecular-weight substances, it is able to stimulate the body defense mechanism and produce allergic reactions. The phenomenon involving the hapten was demonstrated in 1945 by Drs. Carl Landsteiner and Merrill Chase of the Rockefeller Institute.

Where the insidious flea bite was concerned, we learned that the hapten combined with the collagen of the skin. Collagen, a protein, is really the supporting structure of the body, and is involved in many mechanisms. In another phase of the study, we were able to demonstrate the hypersensitivity to the pest bite. Working mainly with guinea pigs, one flea nip would cause no trouble. Another bite a few days later would set them off—a clear example of delayed hypersensitivity. In challenging the animals with the insect bites, we were able to actually time the very moment of acute sensitivity.

As a result of the flea work, I became very interested in studying the haptenic mechanism in the immune response— the role of small-sized chemicals in the defense processes of the body.

There was a sound reason. *The chemicals man uses as drugs and chemicals used as food additives are both low-molecular compounds, subject to the same behavior as the hapten demonstrated in flea saliva.*

An artificial food color, such as the chemical tartrazine— Food, Drug & Cosmetic (FD & C) "Yellow #5—can behave within the human body in the same manner as a "drug" used for medication—a fact some physicians have overlooked.

Because of this similarity, we extended our research and began to look into the adverse reactions to drugs and food additives in patients who visited the allergy clinic for treatment. Aspirin-sensitive patients became the center of our interest. Like all other drugs, aspirin is capable of both beneficial effects and unwanted reactions. The substance known chemically as acetylsalicylic acid is nonprescription medicine's chief do-it-all. Since the medication is used not only as pure aspirin but in many other over-the-counter products for cold relief, headache and arthritis, adverse reactions are common. It appears to have a slowly building, accumulative effect, finally exploding into full-blown intolerance.

Despite the widespread use of aspirin, dating back to 1899, medical science is just beginning to understand the mystery of how it works, but it may be years before the exact pharmacological mechanism is known. Meanwhile, the doctor can only make a diagnosis for aspirin-sensitivity on the basis of the patient's medical history and simply eliminate the product. There is no "test" for it, and to challenge the sensitivity to aspirin is to run the risk of precipitating shock, even death, in the patient.

Very early in the aspirin studies, we learned from a report by Dr. W. B. Shelley, in the *Journal of the American Medical Association*, that a number of foods contain a natural salicylate radical (or "group," i.e., two or more atoms specifically arranged) which is not necessarily identical with aspirin but is closely allied in basic structure. These common foods have the potential to induce the same type of adverse reaction caused by the manufactured aspirin.

I designed a patient management program which was termed a "salicylate-free" diet. It instructed the patient not only to avoid aspirin but also to eliminate the foods which contain natural salicylates. However, we soon realized that the list of foods was incomplete, so Dr. Alice Friedman, then a resident on my clinic staff, referred to the original German data to identify every food containing the aspirin-like radical: apricots, prunes, peaches, plums, raspberries, grapes, oranges, cucumbers, tomatoes—a rather sizable list. Few people like the idea of giving up a number of otherwise wholesome foods, but patients afflicted with salicylate-sensitivity usually prefer diet to agony.

We also discovered that seven of the synthetic-flavor chemicals widely used in foods contain a salicylate radical.

These were added to the diet's taboo items, which now included various bakery goods, some ice creams, chewing gums, some soft drinks, some gelatin products—anything that was enhanced with the so-called mint flavors. In addition, all synthetic wintergreen, lime and lemon flavors were placed in dietary prison, joining strawberry, raspberry, grape and other manufactured taste-bud products.

Despite the exclusion of aspirin as well as all foods containing the natural salicylates and those with a synthetic salicylate radical, we were still unsuccessful with a number of patients who had confirmed aspirin-sensitivity. It was puzzling.

Then reports by clinical investigators began appearing in medical literature with indications that tartrazine—FD & C "Yellow 5"—could cause reactions in aspirin-sensitive patients. Among the doctors reporting were Fred Speer, Stephen D. Lockey, Guy Settipane, F. H. Chaffee and Max Samter. I also reported the same finding from San Francisco, and we discovered the reverse was true, too: aspirin could produce adverse reactions in patients sensitive to Yellow 5. Yet, most important, aspirin and tartrazine are not structurally related.

Additionally, Speer attributed six cases of asthma to the artificial color. Lockey reported that Yellow 5 had caused hives in three adults after transmittal by dyed medications. Chaffee and Settipane targeted Yellow 5 again for asthma via yellow-coated vitamins.

We were all reporting in medical journals for scientific-information purposes, not to frighten the public or harass the already beleaguered food-color industry.

On the basis of the tartrazine discoveries, I expanded the salicylate-free diet to include all foods as well as drugs that contain the ubiquitous yellow dye. We were now eliminating a vast number of packaged or processed foods, since Yellow 5 has such a wide range in the food supply. Following this procedure, we again improved the response in controlling illnesses due to aspirin-sensitivity, but we still did not achieve complete success in some patients.

Then an observation by two London pharmacologists, Drs. John Vane and Sergio Ferreira, came to my attention. They had demonstrated that aspirin and Indomethacin, a drug used for the treatment of arthritis, have the identical inhibitory effect on the production of a group of mediators in the body. Known as prostaglandins, they are an important family of naturally occurring chemicals in all body tissues, and they participate in a variety of physiological actions.

This information practically leaped off the paper. The Vane-Ferreira finding was the second hard observation that compounds with no structural relationship to aspirin could produce reactions in individuals sensitive to this drug. I then theorized that among the several thousand synthetic chemicals in the food supply, there could be other substances potentially harmful to these particular patients. Though the compounds would in no way resemble aspirin, the chemicals had the ability to cross-react.

On the basis of this hypothesis, I redesigned the diet once again to include *all foods* and *all drugs* that were artificially dyed; *all foods* and *all drugs* that were artificially flavored, as well as those containing nature's salicylates. It was no longer a "salicylate-free" diet. It went considerably beyond that early program.

From that point on, although the responses were not 100 percent on each occasion—medicine has yet to reach that heady pinnacle—we were overwhelmingly successful in patient management. It was this diet that I prescribed to the

Oakland "hives" patient in 1965 and received the surprising response of a behavioral modification.

We had come a long way—almost fifteen years' worth—from the high-leaping flea, but the low-molecular compounds had come with us.

# 2

# The Role of Allergy

During 1966 and 1967 we found other patients, children as well as adults, with personality disturbances that "might" be linked to synthetic colors and flavors. They all visited the clinic with complaints that appeared to be allergic—itching, hives, skin rashes, asthma.

Though some of the pediatric patients were hyperactive, our main concern was to immediately alleviate complaints suggestive of allergic reactions. We used the diet frequently. Now and then I heard vague reports that behavioral patterns in the children had changed; that disruption at home and in school had almost stopped; that learning ability had improved.

The observations were satisfying to hear, but I was an allergist, not a behaviorist. I reported the findings but did not emphasize them; nor did I make a study of them because such activity was not within the scope of the Allergy

Department. At that time I did not have an intense interest in behavioral problems and I was unaware of the critical situation in hyperkinesis and learning disability that was developing throughout the country.

Unfortunately, no specialty in medicine can keep abreast of developments and information in all the other specialties. As a whole, medicine itself cannot be totally aware of the various social problems which nonetheless are part of the entire health structure. Very often it is a matter of personal interest when the specialist moves out of his field into related areas.

However, within the clinic's allergy unit, interest in food additives had grown yearly. We had traced hives in young patients to the synthetics in chewable vitamins; to the ingestion of a popular summer drink for children, made by mixing water and a fruit-flavored powder. Earlier we had pinpointed cyclamates, the artificial sweeteners, as the cause of five different skin disorders. By 1968 we had diagnosed more than a hundred cases of hypersensitivity to synthetic flavors and colors. In this field, we had the expertise to make solid judgment.

In March of that year I presented a paper, "Recognition of Food Additives as a Cause of Symptoms of Allergy," before the Twenty-fourth Annual Congress of the American College of Allergists, meeting in Denver. I attempted to stress the hazards of some of the additives, citing cases that had occurred throughout the country.

Concerning chemical dyes, I thought it would be of value to the physician and to the general public if the exact name of the dye used in food preparation and pharmaceuticals were to be listed on the label. Current listings are seldom specific. England had already passed such regulations, specifying that the exact color, and also any flavor, be printed under true names.

"U.S. Certified Color" means nothing when you are attempting to treat a patient or avoiding a particular chemical at time of purchase. In medications, it can be critical. My suggestion seemed to be received enthusiastically by allergists, but elsewhere it met with apparent apathy. Or perhaps precise labeling would involve too much government and corporate bother. In any case, the problem continues to grow monthly with those individuals who react adversely to the synthetic dyes and flavors.

Initially, I felt these reactions were allergic in nature. Allergy is concerned with the defense processes of the body, but the term has wandered far astray from its scientific interpretation. In common speech, allergy has now become synonymous with any form of intolerance or even dislike. "Allergic" is frequently used when an individual doesn't care for a food, though he may tolerate it easily. "I'm allergic to onions, plastic pillows and Sam" usually means that the person simply detests onions, plastic pillows and poor Sam. Even in medicine, the general practitioner or the specialist outside the allergy field sometimes forgets that everything that looks or acts like allergy may not be allergy.

Until Drs. Samter and Farr convincingly demonstrated that the adverse reactions to aspirin were nonallergic in nature, it was generally held to be an allergic mechanism. Following their work, I too became a convert to the nonallergic concept of aspirin sensitivity.

Since patients who are aspirin-sensitive may also react to the artificial colors and flavors, I saw the possibility that the nonallergic theory might apply to these synthetic food additives. My clinical observations over a period of ten years, together with the research of others in the field, seem to support the contention: the adverse reaction to artificial colors and flavors is nonallergic.

Whether the patient is an adult or a hyperkinetic child, there is no natural body defense against the synthetic additives.

# 3

# Behavior Linked to
# Artificial Colors and Flavors

Illness makes no distinction between physician or secretary, lawyer or coal miner. In the late sixties I was struck down by a serious internal ailment and underwent several grueling operations. My activities had to be slowed down during the long recuperation, and I eventually became Chief Emeritus of the Allergy Department. Don German, a talented young doctor whom I had brought into the department, took over operational duties that now serviced five or six thousand patients in nine hospitals. We had grown considerably since 1951.

I didn't think too much about the "physician, heal thyself" aspect, but I suppose the writing of a textbook, *Introduction to Clinical Allergy*, was good therapy during the period of recuperation. There seemed to be a need for an elementary presentation on allergy and immunology, something for the student and even the general practitioner. So I was deeply engrossed in this project for two years, going

15

back over my own experiences in the field, researching, ferreting out latest developments.

At last I finished the book and was beginning to think more and more about a life of ease. I had a long and very satisfying medical career. Our orchids, at a weekend and summer home down on the Peninsula, needed tending. I take great joy in watching things grow, seeing the plums and peaches blossom in the spring; finding a green spike on a cymbidium, knowing it will soon bring forth beautiful flowers. I thought of all this. I also wanted to do some reading and, perhaps, to travel a bit.

Then I discovered, or rediscovered, hyperkinesis–learning disability (H-LD), one of the current scientific terms for excessive physical activity coupled with lack of concentration and learning difficulties. Also known as minimal brain dysfunction (MBD), some educators wisely prefer to name it specific learning disability (SLD) to avoid stigma. (For the same reason, some state legislatures call it a "neurological handicap." Children with this problem are not mentally retarded or psychotic.)

No one term describes these children accurately, but it is estimated that at least four million and perhaps as many as five million, in the United States alone, are afflicted with H-LD in varying degrees, mild symptoms to uncontrollable. Other untold hundreds of thousands, perhaps millions, of children throughout the world share the plight. An estimated 50 percent of the diagnosed H-LDs/MBDs in America are on daily drugs as a matter of management.

Attention had long been paid to the H-LD in specialized medical and educational publications, and in panel discussions in both fields. "Hyperkinetic Impulse Disorder in Children's Behavior Problems," one of the early comprehensive studies, appeared in 1957.* Other related papers had been published in the forties and even in the thirties, but they often covered confirmed brain-damage cases or mentally retarded children.

A sharp increase in interest in the problem was noted in the sixties, apparently paralleling the increase of the specific H-LD problem. Those directly involved—children, family, teacher, school administrator, educational institution, researcher, individual family doctor, pediatrician, psychologist, psychiatrist—well knew the struggle. But the general public, myself very much included, did not really become aware of its enormity until 1971 and 1972, when no fewer than thirty-five medical papers, articles and books, all on a professional level, were published within a matter of months. General-circulation magazines began to probe the H-LD dilemma. Newspapers covered the story outside of the medical columns. Television and radio focused on it. *Life* magazine, one barometer of mass interest, devoted seven pages to the H-LD child in 1972. There was astonishment that "millions," as *Life* estimated, were in trouble.

Reviewing the mixture of medical and general-interest publications from the serenity and safety of my apartment study high over the Golden Gate, I was alarmed, if not shocked, by the depth of the problem, the soaring incidence, the frightening but often necessary drug management, the despair noted by both parent and teacher.

Suddenly, retirement did not interest me. I launched into educating myself on the problems surrounding the hyperkinetic child.

The recognition that children exhibit various symptoms

* M. W. Laufer, E. Denhoff and G. Solomons, in *Psychosomatic Medicine*.

associated with H-LD, MBD, or whatever one chooses to call it, is not new. Some suggestive descriptions appear in medical literature as early as 400 B.C. In 1896 a British ophthalmologist, N. Pringle Morgan, and a school physician, James Kerr, reported on cases of reading disability in "intelligent children," one of them using the term "congenital word blindness."

The World War I epidemic of encephalitis, or inflammation of the brain, affected a large number of children. Much attention was directed to the symptoms in the wake of encephalitis. The residual patterns of many children who were ravaged by it were similar to the symptoms now associated with H-LD. Yet, there was no associated significant impairment of intelligence in either instance.

During this period the concept "minimal brain damage" appears to have crept into medical terminology. The children were not mentally retarded, nor was there concrete evidence of brain damage. The brain-damage label gathered strength from 1938 to 1955 with the writings of A. A. Strauss and collaborators, who freely made the association on the basis of clinical similarity.

Then, mercifully, it was altered to "minimal brain dysfunction." Even this stigmatizing term should be outlawed, in my opinion. People uncertain of the terminology often twist it back to "brain damage." Unaware of the differences, newspaper editors sometimes headline stories about a child with the jolting epithet "brain damaged."

In 1962 the Oxford International Study Group in Child Neurology made two recommendations:

1. The term "minimal brain damage" should be reserved for cases with absolute brain pathology; the term "minimal brain dysfunction" should be applied in the absence of demonstrable organic damage.

2. An attempt should be made to classify the heterogeneous patterns encountered in these children.

The Easter Seal Research Foundation sponsored another important conference at the University of Illinois in 1963, at which time adoption of the Oxford proposals on minimal brain dysfunction was recommended, plus the need to classify the children into more precise syndromes.

The result has been the grouping of many syndromes, including "hyperkinesis–learning disability" under the one roof of MBD. It is not an adequate roof.

After studying much of the current literature on the subject by such experts as C. Keith Conners, Eric Denhoff, M. W. Laufer, Paul Wender, Roscoe Dykman, Leon Eisenberg, Virginia Douglas, Robert Sprague, Barbara Fish, and others, I attempted to arrive at a judgment regarding the cause of the disturbance, the different patterns observed, the treatments recommended. Much confusion and many differences of opinion existed, giving birth to continuing controversy.

The first half of my almost fifty years as a physician were spent as a pediatrician. During this pediatric experience, in private practice, as a teacher at Northwestern University Medical School, as chief of pediatrics at Cedars of Lebanon Hospital in Los Angeles, as attending pediatrician and allergist at Los Angeles' Children's Hospital and Los Angeles County Hospital, I had had exposure to thousands of children with a great variety of ailments. Yet I had no recollection of a high frequency of hyperactivity and behavioral problems through all these years. I had seen psychotic children, mentally retarded children, battered children, epileptic children, deeply troubled adolescents, but very few of what might be diagnosed as "classic H-LDs." However, since

1945 my practice had been limited to clinical allergy, administration and research, so, regretfully, I had lost contact, for the main part, with general pediatric problems during the critical H-LD "explosion" years.

But one very early experience kept drifting through my mind. As a graduate student at the Pirquet Clinic in Vienna in 1928 (pediatric residencies were not common in the United States in that period), I became friendly with a young Austrian physician, Bernard Dattner, who conducted a seizure clinic in Vienna. He required all patients to maintain a strict diet diary, since he believed he could correlate the incidence and severity of seizures with the ingestion of certain foods. Results appeared to justify his procedures. Of course, additives were not involved, for the simple reason that there were few in the Viennese food supply, but diet control was very much involved. In thinking of the H-LDs, I kept coming back to Dattner's work.

In addition, of course, I thought about the child allergy patients I had treated whose behavior had unexpectedly responded to the elimination diet; I remembered the Oakland woman who had been a terror in her home and at work, and had changed dramatically in ten days, following diet management.

By now I was positive that no serious consideration, in cause and effect, diagnosis and treatment of the H-LD, had been given to environmental factors such as additives. Everything from toxemia and drugs during pregnancy; asphyxia and jaundice at birth; brain damage during delivery; genetic variations; retarded development of the nervous system; endocrine disturbances had been offered as possible causes. Perhaps a "forest and trees" situation existed; perhaps some explanations were as close as the kitchen cupboard.

I went over and over what I knew about immunology.

Was it possible that the artificial flavorings and colorings were causing the behavioral disturbances? The time factor favored it. The additives, particularly the flavorings, had not been used in any great quantity until after World War II. Most of the synthetic additives, aside from colors, were less than thirty-five years old. Could the mass of convenience foods, the great tangle of additives, have anything to do with the recent alarming incidence of H-LD?

There seemed to be circumstantial evidence. A Standard & Poor's graph projecting the dollar-value increase in artificial flavors looked very much like a graph indicating the rising trend of H-LD for the same period. A soft-drink graph displayed a certain parallel to the increased incidence in hyperactive children, and the synthetics were often used in the soft beverages.

Soon I began to talk about these observations with other doctors and with friends. Word got around that I had a theory about the hyperkinetic–learning disabled child. One noon in late October 1972 I found myself before the cameras of KPIX-TV, San Francisco, discussing what I had learned of the H-LD and talking about my slowly hardening hypothesis that synthetic food additives might, in some unknown way, be tampering with the brain and nervous system by short-circuiting some functions *in a particular group of children* genetically predisposed to these chemicals.

The mother of a boy I shall call Johnny A was not tuned to KPIX that day, but a friend saw the telecast. In a few days, Johnny A's mother called Kaiser to ask if she might have an appointment.

# 4

# Four Hyperactive Boys

Deliberately running his tricycle into the path of an on-coming car was the single most dangerous activity Johnny A undertook, but his home and kindergarten repertoire of aggression and unhappiness included stomping, kicking walls while in temper tantrums, general surliness, telling big lies about small problems and creating chaos hazardous to the stability of those around him.

This handsome boy, who lived in a small town some sixty miles from the Golden Gate, had begun to manifest the rather bizarre behavior patterns when he was about five. He was either "up" or "down," wild beyond control or placid to the point of being dull, seldom staying in the mid-range of the normal child. Yet he seemed normal in all physical aspects, and he was intelligent beyond the average. At the same time, he couldn't concentrate, couldn't learn.

Beginning in late spring 1971, the aggressive periods lasted from outbursts of a few minutes to prolonged sieges of several days. However, there were times when his parents could truthfully describe him as a "model child." Then, without warning, he would shift inner gears and turn into a small, terrifying Mr. Hyde.

After a year of endurance and frustration, the boy's mother finally decided to seek medical help. She had a hunch, deserving of any doctor's consideration, that large amounts of carbohydrates, sugar from any source, might be triggering the hyperactivity and aggression. Her fair-haired, wiry son loved soft drinks, candy and cake—not exactly abnormal for any healthy child. He also seemed to go completely wild after birthday parties and during family gatherings around holidays. Many children react to the party-family feast-holiday excesses, but this boy sometimes maintained the pattern for days afterward. Whatever the maternal instincts, Johnny A was a likely candidate for hyperkinesis.

Now six years old, he was admitted to the University of California Medical Center, Department of Pediatrics, San Francisco, for observation, referred by the family physician.

On June 2, 1972, a psychiatrist, director of the Child Study Unit, interviewed the parents and Johnny's twelve-year-old brother, who was not similarly afflicted. It was a difficult interview. The style of the family was one of quiet control. *Everything's in order.* "Goodness" was stressed repeatedly, and the psychiatrist wondered if Johnny was not paying a high price for the familial commitment to "goodness."

But the mother remembered that Johnny had been somewhat difficult since infancy, even with regard to comforting and cuddling. The father recalled exasperation in handling Johnny since crib days. The psychiatrist then quickly established that the problem really dated back long before the ingestion of large amounts of sugar, and decided that family stress might well be playing a major role in the behavior. He recommended counseling for all of them.

At first the mother insisted that family stress was not at fault—blame always being difficult to accept when specifics cannot be fingered. She still believed that "sugar" was the archcriminal. A maternal great-grandmother had diabetes mellitus, she revealed. Her own health was better on a high-protein, low-carbohydrate diet.

A subsequent thorough physical examination of the child offered no solid clues. The routine blood and urine tests were normal. He had a six-hour glucose tolerance test, followed by a six-hour sucrose tolerance test. There was no evidence of the suspected hypoglycemia, or low blood sugar.

An electroencephalographic (EEG) study was conducted and it appeared that a pattern in the frontal lobe of the brain might be interpreted as a form of epilepsy. Yet Johnny had no record of seizures, the usual evidence of epilepsy.

A drug was administered for the purpose of exaggerating the brain pattern, with inconclusive results. No additional abnormality was uncovered, and the initial EEG was left open to question. This was not the first time that a hyperkinetic child had baffled the EEG.

But something was definitely wrong with Johnny A! Children do not usually steer tricycles toward moving autos or disrupt entire classrooms. The psychiatric appraisal was that no "school phobia," sometimes thought to be a key to erratic classroom conduct, was involved. School phobia occurs frequently, and usually fleetingly, and means "acute anxiety" as much as anything. Dread of school, for one reason or another, is not uncommon, but Johnny didn't "dread" school.

From a neurological standpoint, he appeared to be completely normal, yet all the symptoms pointed elsewhere. The doctors were left with "family stress" as an unwelcome diagnosis, and the pediatrician involved finally recommended that the family concentrate on that for two months, prior to the starting of school in the fall.

If results weren't satisfactory, then Johnny would be placed on Dilantin, an anticonvulsant drug normally used for epileptic treatment. The possibility of epilepsy had not been entirely discarded. The dosage would be 100 milligrams (mgm) daily. Everything that had been done up to that point seemed justified; it was sound clinical procedure.

During July and August, Johnny's family attempted to reduce whatever stress there was within the home. However, as parents of so many H-LDs have discovered, stress cannot be reduced when the major cause of the disturbance, the small Hyde, is climbing the walls. Action usually triggers reaction, regardless of the degree of parental affection and sympathy.

Naturally, his parents were frightened at the prospect of years ahead with drug control of a problem to which there seemed to be no solution. They had heard about other H-LDs on drug management. At age six, Johnny A faced the grim daily routine of pill-popping.

Johnny B was seven years and three months old when his mother took him to a pediatrician because of behavior problems. He was diagnosed as having "classic hyperkinesis and soft neurologic signs," the latter stemming from an inability to coordinate. He had trouble buttoning his shirt, eyes and hands not seeming to communicate.

The boy was immediately placed on Ritalin, the CIBA-Geigy Corporation trade name for methylphenidatehydrochloride, a stimulant drug commonly used in the management of H-LDs. Dosage was 40 mgm daily. The September school term was about to begin.

The response to the drug was "extraordinarily good." In fact, it was almost too good—Johnny B became a zombie. The drug was reduced to 10 mgm daily and then Johnny did rather well in school, both in class work and behavior.

Soon, however, there was a black rubber stamp, CONFERENCE, on his progress report from the school he attended on the outskirts of San Francisco. The teacher wanted to talk about Johnny B because, apparently, he was now failing to respond to the drug.

On January 17, 1973, the school reported: "Excessive fidgetiness, extreme distractibility; inability to adjust to new situations and irritability. The child talks constantly when he should be listening." Another note said: "He should be aware of *us*."

Johnny B was caught squarely in the H-LD trap. His drug program was increased to 20 mgm a day. They'd try that for a while.

At three years and six months, Johnny C was placed on Ritalin management. Almost since infancy, he had been described as "unhappy, extremely hyperactive and uncontrollable." He was unable to focus his attention on any project for more than two or three seconds.

Ritalin, the stimulant, has a mystifying paradoxical effect on many child patients—it seems to quiet them down. Johnny C reacted promptly, calming down and becoming less distractible. He exhibited a better degree of "self-control" and seemed more inclined to respond to routine demands.

At age five, Johnny C started school and immediately

ran into learning difficulties. He couldn't grasp numbers and the alphabet, although everyone knew he was a bright boy. He frequently created havoc in the classroom and couldn't get along with his fellow students.

Johnny and his family struggled for the next two and a half years. So did his teachers, classmates and the few neighborhood playmates he was able to retain. When he was seven and a half, Stelazine, a tranquilizer, was added to his therapy for greater control during school hours.

The Stelazine presumably calmed him down when the Ritalin didn't do its job. Additionally, the tranquilizer aided in sleeping patterns, which had always been uneven; it seemed to add more control over minor muscular movements.

The parents were anguished. Their seven-year-old son had already been on drugs for four years. Now he was taking another drug. He was totally dependent on them. What next? Still another drug?

Johnny D was not a child. He was a tall, well-developed young man of seventeen. A quick glance would indicate that he was completely normal, but his symptoms of hyperactivity dated back to infancy. He'd rocked the crib constantly, even to the point of breaking it up. He'd had difficulty sleeping; the slightest noise would arouse him. He reacted like a tense fox.

Dexedrine, which is an amphetamine, was started when he was eight years old. At the age of thirteen, Ritalin was substituted for Dexedrine. Then a Stelazine program was initiated, simultaneously, as in the case of Johnny C.

Now, at seventeen, the strapping young man from an outlying community of San Francisco, was on 50 mgm of Ritalin and 4 mgm of Stelazine daily, divided into doses before school, at noon and in late afternoon.

In 1962, when Johnny D was six, his teacher had reported: "—— is a disorganized child. He is poorly coordinated and will not attempt to participate in any musical activity. He has a short attention span and wants your attention when he can get it. —— is not able to relate to other children; he is not able to share or take turns and seems completely at a loss in the classroom. He is unable to follow through on anything he starts."

Not much had changed eleven years later. His parents were both educators, very intelligent people, but Johnny couldn't read or write very well. They'd been told that the problem would likely "go away" when he reached puberty. Somewhat past that magic-cure period, he was now two years behind in his class, and though the hyperactivity was not as marked, he still couldn't coordinate. His younger sister showed no signs of the malady. His teacher-parents tried to hide their frustrations, concern and deep disappointment, but their teen-age son had every chance of failing in life.

I have, of course, concealed the true names of these boys who have taken so much punishment from their nervous systems, and tragically, from society. Through the failure of society to understand the nature of their disturbances, they have already been stigmatized. Unavoidably, the initials MBD, H-LD or SLD encircle them. The classifications have every chance of following them throughout their entire school experience, possibly into later life.

I worked with over a hundred such children, and their stories are somewhat the same. I observed them, talked to their parents, studied their medical and psychological reports, and examined them. I was eager to help them out of their hyperkinetic traps, and particularly eager to suggest a way to eliminate drug management.

# 5

# Diet Controls Hyperactivity

## JOHNNY A

Reference Johnny A, my office record for November 17, 1972, begins: "This six-year-old white male reported to the Allergy Department with a complaint of behavioral problems. Details of the history are on the enclosed report from the University of California and from the child's pediatrician."

The UC Medical Center report was routine: "Physical examination revealed a cooperative articulate male in no acute distress. Blood pressure 95/75, height 121 cm (50th percentile), weight 23.3 kg, temperature 27, pulse 88, respiration 20. The skin is clear. Examination of the head, eyes, ears, nose and throat is essentially within normal limits, etc."

I examined him again and found that physically, he was fine.

He now sat rather quietly, looking around the office, not paying much attention to his mother or myself. I had expected a small wild man. He was a beautiful child, and as the UC report had said, for the moment "a cooperative articulate male." He did not act hyperkinetic and it was difficult for me to picture him guiding a tricycle into a car.

I asked his mother if he was currently on medication. The answer was negative. She hated drugs. Forty-two years old, she matched the psychiatrist's description of the family. She was calm and very determined. She still did not accept "family stress" as the reason for Johnny's behavior. She firmly believed that what he ate and drank was the principal cause of his problem. Responding to the remarks I'd made on TV, she'd already restricted the intake of many foods containing additives—all soft drinks, candies and cakes—and had noted a great improvement in her son.

"Listen to the grandmother." Or mother. Or father. This advice was given to me long ago in Chicago by my mentor, Dr. Isaac Abt, a world-renowned pediatrician. I had used the admonition frequently throughout my career, and though it didn't always work, this time it was applicable. I accepted the mother's contention, first expressed to UC doctors six months previously, that what Johnny ate and drank was "turning him on."

I said, "All right, let's put him on the diet."

There was no danger. No drugs were involved. The diet had been used thousands of times. Chiefly, it eliminated many junk foods. I was simply enabling the mother to go several steps further than she'd already gone, to attempt total management by elimination of suspected "turn-ons."

The mother was worried about meeting Johnny A's insatiable "sweet tooth" demands. I suggested her own kitchen: homemade candy, homemade ice cream; home made pastries, steering clear of the synthetic colors and flavors. Then I requested that she keep a strict "diet diary" of everything the child ate or drank so that she could judge his behavior against infractions, either voluntary or by mistake.

The next day, a Saturday, Johnny A began rigid food-and-beverage management. His dedicated mother, a remarkable woman, began a diary that lasted, with few breaks, until April 16, 1973.

Her comments, page by page, proved to be of value. On the 18th, Johnny had spaghetti for dinner. The sauce was homemade. She wrote: "I goofed. Used tomato sauce but there was no obvious behavior change."

*Perhaps he can eventually have tomatoes,* I thought. *They contain a natural salicylate but he might be able to tolerate them.*

Tuesday, the 21st, she underlined chocolate bar. "At 11:30. Very noticeable behavior change at 2:30 P.M."

*From that incident on, a pattern developed. Any candy infraction (store-bought), ingested singly, appeared to cause a reaction in two to three hours.*

Wednesday. A question mark. "Something off diet here. Slight behavior change."

*I checked the items. Perhaps the breakfast bacon was artificially flavored with hickory.*

On Thanksgiving Day, Johnny A had the full traditional dinner of turkey, cranberry sauce, pumpkin pie. Also on the table were pickled watermelon rinds and pickled peaches. "These eaten with a full dinner and no change noted."

*Interesting. I wondered what would happen if he were to eat them on an empty stomach.*

32

A week later she reported: "Distinct appetite increase these days."

A day after that, Johnny got another candy bar on the sly, about 2 P.M. He admitted it later. "One quick outburst about 4 P.M. and not again until the next day. Again, short and quick outburst which I was able to talk him out of."

December 1: "1 teaspoon of antihistaminic cough syrup at bedtime produced a raving maniac the early part of December 2."

*I knew the brand. It was both synthetically flavored and synthetically colored.*

December 19: "School party—Popcorn only, refused all other candies. Generally good behavior."

December 20: "Party at school. Cupcake. He says store-bought. 1 cookie, with candies on top. Slight behavior change."

Throughout the Christmas holidays, usually a disaster for Johnny, he stayed on the diet. His mother noted: "Good behavior."

On the 27th: "½ of unknown candy bar and bubble gum. Noticed behavior change before I learned of foods eaten."

At year's end Johnny was doing fine; then, scarlet fever. And trauma. "Pediatric prescription, antibiotic. Yellow color. A hassle to keep from getting liquid prescription."

*An old hassle. Practically all pediatric medicines are artificially colored and flavored.*

January 2: "Changed to *white* antibiotic."

His behavior throughout the first part of the illness was "cranky, crabby—nothing could please him." This was quite normal for any ill child, but by January 8 she noted: "No food record but all within diet. He was still home. Behavior great."

On January 20 his mother experimented with orange juice. "Off-diet! He misses this the most of all the items he can't have. He was doing so well I thought I'd give it a try. Talked like a magpie. Behavior problem maybe. Questionable."

March 1: "Hamburger with relish. Juice punch. Popsicle. Had his own money supposedly for plain burger and chips. Super-charged behavior."

*I suspected the punch and Popsicle. I was now convinced that it only took an infinitesimal amount to trigger reaction.*

March 2: "Still affected. Very crabby."

March 3: "Behavior okay again."

*Johnny's reaction displayed a pattern that was to be observed in later patients. The reactions would last from twenty-four to seventy-two hours.*

March 29: "Punch and homemade chocolate cupcakes (served at school)—no knowledge of ingredients used. Behavior change noted. More of a bad temper with great flourishes. He hit his head quite badly in the process."

The next day: "Note written to school to request no extra food for him without my permission—verbal requests don't seem to be obeyed."

It appeared to me that the pattern was definitely one of "turn-on" and "turn-off" by what he ingested, supporting the earlier fragmentary evidence of the children who came to the clinic with possible allergy problems. Almost six months of detailed reporting by this mother connected certain foods and certain beverages to behavior patterns, in my opinion.

Her general comments were also of interest: "Potato chips, although not listed in ingredients, must have something extra added as I note an improvement since we have stopped their use."

*Other children have also reacted to potato chips, though it appears that only the barbecue-flavor variety are significant.*

Her questions also indicated the problems of any mother attempting to use the elimination-diet management: "Caramel color? Is this off-diet? Dried onion soup has this ingredient, as do other cooking helpers. Bouillon cubes? Are these okay? Soy sauce?"

*Caramel color may be artificial. Dried onion soup and bouillon cubes are often artificially colored and flavored. Frequently, soy sauce is flavored, but there is at least one good unflavored brand on the market. Little of specific value can be learned from the labels. Nonetheless, they must be checked.*

In late April the mother of Johnny A summed up the experience of six months: "There has been a general overall improvement, but I don't like his conduct at school. The teacher said there is an improvement in him, as I told you last time. He is head and shoulders over the rest of his class in his abilities but the quality seems rather erratic. I am fully aware of the fact that some of these things are learned from his past behavior; that although the cause is gone, the action still remains. It is this part that I have been working on with him—trying to undo some of the patterns of action—not listening and not minding are two of the largest areas."

Her appraisal was quite correct. The child cannot adjust overnight, nor in a few weeks. This is particularly true in relations with peers. They expect him to be the "horrible" Johnny of the past.

I discussed Johnny A with my colleagues Alice Friedman

and Don German, quite casually. They were both skeptical. So was I—the response might have been a psychological reaction to the diet program and to the constant attention and vigilance of the parents. Yet, I was encouraged. *The boy had shown improvement.*

As a very conventional medical doctor, I have always been leery of "cure" by diet. The fad diets, on which you lose five pounds a week, make me uneasy if not frightened. However, I also know that good food control is good health control. Additionally, I had reason to believe that some children would gain weight on this diet. Many hyperkinetics desperately need a few more pounds.

## JOHNNY B

By now I had begun to reach out for other H-LDs. I was not satisfied with accidental encounters resulting from TV interviews. Among the new patients was Johnny B, who had been referred by the Kaiser Pediatric Department. He was eight, and on 20 mgm of Ritalin daily, the initial dosage of 40 mgm, prescribed the past August, having turned him into a "zombie." His behavior and learning problems had not improved since the school had called his mother in for conference in January.

On March 21, in my office, she talked of the boy's infancy. From seven weeks on, he had been bothered by colds, a sore throat and a perennial cough. She attached significance to a "green pill," which she could not identify, given to her during pregnancy to prevent a rapid weight gain. The delivery had been normal.

On April 3, two weeks after their initial visit, I reviewed Johnny's sample daily meal chart. It was loaded with additives, plus a colored, chewable vitamin. I tested him for allergy. Although he reacted to two environmental factors, tests performed on his back, I did not think they were linked to hyperactivity. That day I placed him on the K-P Diet (K-P stands both for Kaiser-Permanente and for kitchen police, of which a certain amount is required).

As of April 17, the record said of Johnny B: "Diet has been carefully observed with the exception of two infractions: (1) lollipop, (2) strawberries. Mother reports improvement in behavior. Mother reports adverse reaction to Ritalin last three times. Seems to be ineffective."

*I wondered if some mechanism was working here. Was the elimination diet inducing an intolerance to the drug?*

Ten days later I wrote: "Has improved in reading. Is considered for a higher group. Mother reports he is quieter. Diet reviewed. If possible, reduce Ritalin to 10 mgm every 48 hours or 5 mgm every 24 hours."

On May 3, his mother, knowing that we would soon phase Ritalin out entirely, sent a note to school to check his progress, informing them of the imminent drug stoppage: "He seems more relaxed at home without medication and I hope he is the same in class."

The note came back with two messages: "In class, he's great. He's too smart in his reading group. We're skipping him."

Then there was a sentence from his playground supervisor: "Sorry, at this time he is having trouble in the yard, fighting, beating up, etc." Once again, it was too much to expect the boy to change completely overnight. He'd only been on the diet for a month and he was withdrawing from medication simultaneously. His peers likely remembered him as a bully and reacted to his past patterns. Counterreaction was very probable.

Still, since his classroom behavior had improved, as

well as his schoolwork and home behavior, we were far ahead. I decided to go all the way and discontinued Ritalin totally on May 11.

With absolutely no drug support, the next three weeks were very erratic, both in the classroom and on the playground. Schoolwork, however, continued to improve rapidly. The home behavior remained good. There was no reason to panic and place him back on drugs.

Johnny B continued to have many problems, but by the end of the term, in early June, he was making it. Although there was something still to be desired in his habits and attitude, his report gave him a "satisfactory" in oral reading and understanding and a "very good" in number work. To me, it was an indication that the youngster's nervous system was allowing him to concentrate. Concentration might well allow him to change "habits and attitude."

The last notation I had was September 8: "Continued improvement. Check pediatric outpatient record."

## JOHNNY C

Johnny C was a "Kaiser" baby, born in the health plan's Santa Clara hospital, so there was easy access to his records. *Character of labor was normal. Response of the infant, normal. Complications, none.*

Yet, as we have seen, at the appalling age of three and a half, Johnny C had been put on Ritalin for classic hyperkinesis. I noted that during the past year, when the boy was seven, the tranquilizer Stelazine had been added to exert additional control.

Though I didn't see him at the time, he had been admitted to the allergy clinic in 1968, when tests indicated need for an allergen to control a skin disorder. He was readmitted in 1970 for another possible allergy but the diagnosis was "asymptomatic and no skin reactivity." As far as hyperkinesis was concerned, his allergy history had no significance.

I listened to his mother tell a story of problems since the age of twelve or sixteen weeks. They hadn't stopped. The combination of Ritalin and Stelazine had helped to control muscular and nervous movements as well as school behavior, but not, unfortunately, learning ability. During regular school sessions, Johnny was in a special class for the learning disabled; during summer he was in a normal class. Almost year round he went to school in a small, private hell.

We discussed the possibility of the diet and I requested a two-week record of what he was eating and drinking. Meanwhile I started the child on a battery of allergy tests because of past conditions. The results were negative.

When the sample food list was returned I wasn't too surprised to find it filled with artificial colors and flavors. I put eight or ten check marks on the first page of three meals.

On July 2 Johnny C began the K-P Diet, and on July 8, a startling six days later, his mother reported: "He's become very quiet, less irritable; easy to control."

On July 13 I noted: "Changed child. More self-control than on Ritalin. Able to reason with parents and peers. Less distractible. Decreased Ritalin to once a day, at 7 A.M.; Stelazine only at night."

On the 15th, Johnny C ate a bakery doughnut at 7 A.M. and by 10 A.M. was "hyperactive, unable to use self-control." Twenty-four hours later, after the food had cleared his system, he was back to the "new normal."

On July 17 I stopped the Stelazine. Five days later, when Johnny C and his mother returned to the clinic, I stopped all medication. There had been an unbelievable improvement in a period of fifteen days. I wondered how often the diet would show such a favorable response.

I called Don German into the office and said, "Doctor, I won't even talk. I'll let the mother tell you everything."

On July 27 Johnny C sneaked some candy and turned into a whirling dervish for twenty-four hours. *Predictable*, I thought.

I felt very good. After four and a half years, Johnny C was off drugs and the only possible answer for it, in my opinion, was the elimination of the colors and flavors. The "turn-on" and "turn-off" pattern was again indicated by the ingestion of the doughnut and candy, even to the timing of two or three hours—hyperactivity in action again.

## JOHNNY D

Johnny D, at the age of seventeen, didn't at all like the idea of seeing still another doctor. He'd had a steady round of them for years and was currently in psychotherapy. His animosity was hardly veiled on the September afternoon he came to my office. For my part, in the more than twenty-five cases I had studied thus far, I had not been in contact with a seventeen-year-old hyperkinetic. I was interested to see what would happen.

The teen-ager's educator father had heard me speak about the K-P Diet to a group of parents and teachers in his community. That night I said I'd been able to discard "Ritalin and Stelazine management in *some* children." The father was skeptical and it was not until after he'd learned of the success with Johnny C that he called for an appointment. Ritalin had not worried him, but Stelazine was something else, in his opinion. Since Johnny C was off Stelazine . . .

A confidential report on Johnny D, prepared for the San

40

Francisco Unified School District, had concluded: "Results of psychological evaluation indicated a minimally impaired, neurologically handicapped child." It recommended he be placed in a disability class.

I had winced on reading the report. The young man had been fumbling around in school for eleven years and *now* they were ready for a disabled class!

I examined him, and although there were suggestions of allergic disease, otherwise he was a very healthy but un coordinated physical specimen. His mind? I didn't know.

On October 8, a very short time after his first visit, I was pleased to record: "This boy has been able to discontinue all medications after two weeks' dietary control. He will be observed for scholastic achievements and improved muscular coordination. Only time will determine to what degree he has been conditioned over ten years of hyperkinesis; many years of medication. To continue with diet."

On December 26, a good post-Christmas present: "There continues to be improvement in this boy. His outward appearance and expression are more alert and happier. His skin appears clearer. He is most cooperative on the diet. His performance at school is still below his age. However, considering everything, the response is gratifying. Add tomatoes to his diet list."

Then I added something for myself: *Happy New Year.*

## JILL A

For reasons unknown, there appear to be more male hyperkinetics than female. Estimates vary, according to observers, on a ratio of one female to every nine males, as a low, or four females to every ten males, as a high. At first I thought there was a ratio of one to every nine or ten. However, it appears that more females may be involved than originally estimated.

Jill A, twelve years old, was the patient of a Southern California pediatrician, who had first observed her in August 1970. His diagnosis was: "Hyperactivity with the usual symptoms encountered in the male." The girl had a short attention span, low tolerance for failure and frustration, and slow speech development. At home she could not be disciplined. Socially, she was a flop.

Because she had been adopted, few details of her early infancy were available. Her parents did say that she was already on a vitamin product when she came into their lives, and the vitamin subsequently identified by her pediatrician as a colored-flavored variety.

Jill A was placed on Ritalin therapy in September 1970, and the dosage per day was soon increased. Improvement at home and in school was almost immediate. By December, however, the drug had lost its effectiveness and was discontinued. A month later she was back on it, and the pediatrician reported little gain: "The child is still antagonistic and fails to cooperate with peer groups."

Dosage was increased the following December and continued at a high level until September 10, 1973. At that time, despite the increased dosage, Jill was "extremely aggressive with other children, with a low tolerance level. She lashes out at other children with very little cause. She is forgetful."

She was placed on the elimination diet on that September date, and within two weeks the pediatrician discontinued Ritalin. Another dramatic response to the K-P Diet was noted, but I again felt it would not be the average response. Despite the earlier quick successes, a month on the diet seemed a better estimate if there was going to be a response at all. I was wrong.

If this program works at all, minor or even major response is usually noted within ten days or two weeks—with the exception of children on Dextroamphetamine spansules therapy. This drug is released slowly and also clears the system slowly. A three-week response has been noted in these patients.

The doctor's final report on Jill was: "She has lost her aggressiveness and is at present quiet and well adjusted to her environment. It is still too early to evaluate her school performance. However, with the ability of the child to concentrate, this will no doubt show early improvement."

# 6

# A Mother's Diary

Hopefully, extra kitchen preparation, the need to scan labels carefully and occasional medication difficulties required by K-P Diet management will become minor irritants if the hyperactive child shows improvement. Establishing a routine has a way of flattening out problems after a month or so.

However, the first few weeks of diet trial are apt to be erratic. This is particularly true if the child has been on drug therapy for any appreciable time. The following "withdrawal" diary, written by an aware and sensitive mother, day by day, beginning November 12, 1973, should shatter any illusions of instant peace.

This woman was one of a group of San Francisco area parents who agreed to put their H-LD children on dietary control. Judith Keithley, a graduate student who was working on her master's degree and planning to specialize in the MBD area, volunteered to "round them up."

I requested the parents to take the children off medica-

44

tion for a few days to further establish that they were actually hyperkinetic when "off the pills," then start the K-P Diet.

Six-year-old "Billy," when not churned up, is a charmer: small, dark-haired, very bright, and with a devastating smile.

---

DAY 1—Billy cut out pills at noon himself today, so did not give him one tonight. He seems very eager to begin. *Very active.* Seems extremely happy. Does odd things like asking if he could brush his teeth and then smearing toothpaste all over his face. Read to him, after I made him sit down, for 45 minutes without interruption.

---

DAY 2—Extremely active. Hasn't stopped talking and seems happy but easily frustrated over small tasks. He seems charged with energy and activity. Says he feels too lazy to do anything. Cried because he feels he has, in the last two days, ruined his chances for a good report card. Called work at 11 A.M., saying he had a headache and a stomach ache and wanted to leave school. Convinced him to stay. He's loud, utterly wild as the evening wears on. Picking fights with brother. Body and mouth in constant motion. (Think I will die.) Have to isolate him completely from his brothers unless I'm in the room with him. Crying spell before bed. Nobody loves him. Afraid of losing mother.

---

DAY 3—Erratic behavior. Wet his pants in school today. Behavior same as yesterday. Movements quick. He wants to be "good" and sad that he isn't. It's as if he were divided in half—one part of him fighting the other. Tomorrow we start on diet. He's eager to try. Likes the idea of helping other kids go on his diet. God, I hope it works. Goes to sleep much easier than on the pills.

---

DAY 4—Active all day. Unable to sit through TV program but in good humor. Even-tempered. Did little fighting with brothers. Slept until 9 A.M. Unusual.

---

DAY 5—Started this day quietly but by 3 P.M. unable to stop constant body motion and talking. After 3:00, very emotional. Cries easily. Hurt feelings. Very sensitive. But does not last. Next minute he is happy again. Seems vulnerable. On pills he had walls up but now hides very little. Tonight unable to sit through TV program, even though he was enjoying it, without squirming or talking. Cried afterward and said it was such a sad movie. Cried in bed because movie was so sad but now I hear him laughing wildly.

---

DAY 6—Active but able to respond to discipline. Still cries easily. Refused food at school. Seems determined to stay on diet.

---

DAY 7—Cries over everything. Seems to be taking steps backward. Still unhappy at school. Teacher said she would call Dr. Feingold and tell him that diet not working. Billy upset.

---

DAY 8—Crabby, fighting with brother. Sensitive. Put him to bed at 7:30.

---

DAY 9—Billy seems calm. Not as emotional as last few days. Seems mellow. Responds to requests.

---

DAY 10—4½-hour trip to mountains. Lots of excitement. Thanksgiving dinner. Lots and lots of people. Billy behaved beautifully. He was calm, mannerly, orderly, helped carve the turkey. Was patient. Cannot believe he was not on the pill. Even on the pill he was never this good. Seems happy and contented.

---

DAY 11—Billy said, "I feel beautiful today. Happy. My body feels quiet. With the pill I feel quiet but then I feel sleepy and dizzy. Now I feel quiet but I'm not sleepy."

---

DAY 12—Billy was erratic today. Cried easily. Fussy. Hurt finger. Irritable. Could be tired. Hard to be away from home with him now.

---

DAY 13—Billy cried all night over everything. On top of that, his dog is gone. He ate a bologna sandwich today. I'm tired. Have to go to a meeting tonight. I got unglued at Billy. I feel putting too much pressure on him. His teacher, his sitter and me. We are all at him in one way or another, expecting something of him. Poor kid! Must reassure him tomorrow. [His brother] feeling neglected. The sitter exasperated with Billy's crying. Body hurts magnified a thousand times. Christmas coming. No shopping done. Pressures at work. Damn diet!

(My aide talked to the mother this thirteenth day and scribbled on the case file: "Reacting differently to the diet. Mother seems to feel encouraged. Feel Dr. F. made everything sound too simple. Emotional reactions to going off pill seem so strong.")

---

DAY 14—Must try to get emotional problem caused by stopping pill over to his teacher. Billy trying so hard (accidentally threw away papers from teacher). He is showing a great deal of responsibility on this diet. Must praise him tomorrow. So much to do to keep everyone on even keel. Glad do not have a husband and work, too. Couldn't manage it.

---

DAY 15—Billy calmer tonight. Body always calm now (ever since Thanksgiving). I'm getting used to it. In the beginning if he'd get excited I would immediately tense up in fear the diet wasn't working. Crying much less when I put him to bed at 7:30 instead of 8:30. He seems exhausted when I come home at night. Falls right to sleep and have to work hard to wake him up. Unbelievable. Since he was an infant he's slept so little. Billy much more affectionate and responds to directions almost immediately (a miracle). Is more real (no more lying, sneaking, long monologues, and he hasn't done anything outrageous like challenging the train or ripping tiles off the roof, throwing them in the driveway, putting garbage cans on his head). Fights badly with his brother but this will soon change. Diet and all the emphasis on Billy has upset their relationship. Billy has gained three pounds since beginning of diet.

# 7

# The Patterns of Hyperactivity

During my first observations of the hyperactive child, I used a guide entitled *Descriptive Characteristics of Clinical Pattern of H-LD*:

1. *Marked hyperactivity and fidgetiness*
    rocks—jiggles legs
    dances—wiggles hands
   In infancy, this may be manifested by crib-rocking; head-knocking

2. *Compulsive aggression*
    disruptive at home and in school
    compulsively touches everything and everybody
    disturbs other children
    cannot be diverted from an action
    commits acts dangerous to own safety

3. *Excitable—Impulsive*
    behavior is unpredictable

49

panics easily with temper tantrums which are
usually an expression of frustration

4. *Tolerance for failure and frustration is low*
   demands must be met immediately
   cries often and easily

5. *Short attention span—Unable to concentrate*
   flits from one project to another
   is unable to sit through a school project
   is unable to sit through a meal
   is unable to sit through a TV program

6. *Exceptionally clumsy*
   poor muscle coordination
   eyes and hands do not seem to function together
   has trouble buttoning
   difficulty with writing and drawing
   difficulty with playground activity

7. *Poor sleep habits*
   difficult to get to bed
   hard to get to sleep
   awakes easily

8. Normal or high IQ but fails in school

9. Boys are involved 9:1

10. Rarely more than one child in a family

In any one child, they could all be valid symptoms. All
may apply, in varying degrees, in a period of forty-eight
hours, after which none may apply for twelve hours; then
half may apply for the next twenty-four hours. Any four
may apply to one child and not another, though both were
competently diagnosed as H-LDs.

Due to this wide variability, it is difficult to describe the
typical pattern for the child possessed by H-LD/MBD. The

constantly changing situations for any one child and the great differences in clinical patterns among any group explain the argument that exists among psychologists attempting to evaluate and classify these children.

This observation is supported by one of the leading experts, Dr. C. Keith Conners, director of the Child Development Laboratory, Massachusetts General Hospital, Boston. Conners has stated: "Psychological tests are familiar tools in the evaluation of children with known or suspected brain dysfunction. Although tests continue to play a considerable role in clinical evaluation of children with MBD, their exact role and their utility are matters of considerable controversy."

Almost a hundred different, but often similar, H-LD/ MBD symptoms have been listed in medical publications over the years. Undoubtedly a few more will be added before the decade is over. With such variability, there is little wonder that medical science finds it difficult to define specifics and place a precise label on this disturbed child.

The terms "hyperkinesis" and "hyperactivity" imply a fidgety, active child, wiggling, jiggling and running around a room or playground. But not all of the children exhibit these characteristics. Some of them are reasonably quiet. To a degree, they seem to be influenced by age.

However, on closer examination of the quiet H-LD/ MBD, a variable degree of muscle incoordination can usually be detected. The child cannot easily button a coat, or if older, tie shoe laces or participate successfully in sports. When hand-muscle disturbances are combined with eye incoordination, reading disturbances as well as writing and drawing difficulties can occur. This incoordination is the basis for psychological tests such as the Bender-Visuo-Motor-Gestalt, which requires the child to make figures and drawings. Those made by the H-LD/MBD are distorted and fragmentary.

An excellent two-year study by Dr. Virginia L. Douglas, of McGill University, heading up a research group at Montreal Children's Hospital, points up the confusion of diagnosis: "One of the first difficulties in trying to talk about the hyperactive syndrome is the problem of establishing a diagnosis. The literature has relied heavily on clinical descriptions and, to complicate matters further, these descriptions often overlap considerably with those given for children suffering from 'minimal brain dysfunction' and 'specific learning disabilities.' . . .

"However, as we have learned more about hyperactive children, we have come to believe that hyperactivity is only one of a constellation of symptoms."

With hyperkinesis–learning disability a subgrouping of minimal brain dysfunction, the symptoms sometimes overlapping, there is ample cause for continued parental confusion. Perhaps the simplest approach is: not all MBDs are hyperkinetic, while all H-LDs display the hyperactive patterns, minor to major.

Attempts to classify the various clinical patterns into more specific groups have also resulted in a variety of terms that sometimes confront the puzzled parent: choreiform (incoordinate movement) syndrome; developmental clumsiness; congenital aphasia (understanding spoken and written language); congenital auditory imperception (hearing difficulty) and dyslexia (reading and spelling difficulty).

One doctor's diagnosis for a specific patient was "dysfunctions in auditory perception, visual motor integration and body awareness (directionality). Also found to be emotionally immature." Hearing, eye and hand incoordination, and emotional immaturity only skimmed the surface of the problems facing this child.

There is no easy diagnosis.

Confusion is also present in the width and depth of the problem. The estimates of the total number of H-LD/MBDs in the United States still vary from a high of around 5 million to a low of around 1 million, and a very questionable low-low of 500,000. In truth, no one seems to know. The experts clash again.

State and federal figures are of little help because of the tendency to lump all handicapped children, whether they are mentally retarded, deaf, blind, MBD or H-LD, into one category. One federal figure indicates that 3 percent of the total elementary school population is "learning disabled," yet state statistics appear to run considerably higher.

There is also wide disagreement in the annual growth rate. Some psychologists and psychiatrists, as well as prominent educators, believe the increase has generally paralleled the expanding population. Others, with due alarm, claim it has "run away" in the last twenty years. Current estimates appear to favor the latter opinion.

Some pediatricians have practices that almost specialize in the H-LD/MBD. As a confirmed sample, one three-doctor group in Southern California treats around six hundred such children, a large proportion of them on daily medication. A single Toronto pediatrician reportedly has three hundred in his practice, most of them on drug therapy.

As always, there are observers who discount the existence of anything from a round world to the laws of gravity. One day in the fall of 1973 I was amused to read a prominent columnist in the San Francisco *Chronicle*. He headed his column, "How To Invent a Disease," and then said: ". . . MBD has no real existence, except in the minds of doctors and educators. It is just a fancy concept for children who are difficult to teach, who do not respond to the school system. Yet it is a disease which, for the administrators of the schools, *just has to exist*."

He further hinted that there might be some kind of a conspiracy between doctors, educators and drug companies. As far as I am concerned, for the children involved it would be fortunate if their problem were a dark conspiracy rather than the very real difficulty with which they must cope.

However, and unfortunately, the newspaper article was based on a half-truth, or several half-truths. At least one large drug company has co-sponsored symposiums, staffed by experts or educators, advocating the use of drugs to manage the H-LD. Unquestionably, the experts and educators believe what they say, but financial support by a drug firm, which cannot help being very interested in promoting its product, introduces a disquieting element of conflict of interest. The ultimate goal of such symposiums is to persuade parents and doctors to try drug therapy.

Whether in war or epidemic, man has always profited from the human plight. There are some vested interests in the troubles of the H-LD, and it would be foolish to assume that they did not intend to make harvest until the problem is contained. There will always be opportunists, but the problem of the H-LD was not invented by doctors, teachers or drug companies. Those who ride the bandwagon of this plight are in the minority.

There is no doubt that the number of children in this country with learning disabilities is enormous. Many good and legitimate private schools to meet this specific need of the H-LD, as well as other children with learning disabilities, operate coast-to-coast. No state is without its nonprofit association for the learning disabled, and there is a national organization, the Association for Children with Learning Disabilities. At its last meeting this organization drew some eight thousand parents, teachers and other professionals; the size of this convention is probably another barometer of the total problem.

It is difficult to isolate statistically the hyperactive child and his specific learning problems from those of the blind, deaf and mentally retarded. Figures I've seen for the learning disabled–hyperkinetic vary from 4 percent in the St. Louis, Missouri, school system and 5 percent of all the pupils in the South San Francisco school system to 16 percent in San Bruno, California, and 25 percent in Monroe County in upstate New York.

As a possible indication of the recent "explosion," the California Association for the Neurologically Handicapped estimates that during the period 1961 to 1973, roughly, the incidence of H-LD children in the state rose from 2 percent to an average of 20 to 25 percent; in some cases, 40 percent of the entire school population.

Again, it appears to be a matter of variation and "who reports what." The teacher who reports that 25 percent of her class is H-LD might actually be dealing with only two or three children who are true hyperkinetics. Some of the others may be reacting to the stimulus of the bonafide H-LDs and it is not unreasonable to suspect that some teachers are reacting, or overreacting to the same stimulus. Just as there is no accurate yardstick for this problem in medical science, education cannot be expected to employ one.

Even nursery school does not escape the H-LD dragnet. Dr. Richard Bell and Mary Waldrop, of the Child Research

Branch of the National Institute of Mental Health, used "the play of nursery school children to identify hyperkinesis as the most salient clinical problem in this age group, with 11 to 14 percent of this 'normal sampling' of some 200 children requiring special handling."

Reading disabilities among children are frequently an expression of behavioral disturbance induced by hyperactivity. A federal recognition that 7 million elementary and secondary school children are in severe need of special reading assistance would favor the higher estimates for H-LD incidence rather than the conservative 4 or 5 percent.

However, one factor that appears to influence this type of data is the failure to separate, in some cases, hyperkinesis from learning difficulty. They are actually different aspects of the same problem. This is particularly true of dyslexia, the generic word applied to the whole category of reading and spelling difficulty.

On March 22, 1973, Senator Glenn Beall, of Maryland, presented the following to a special Senate committee:

*An estimated 18.5 million American adults are functional illiterates.*

*In large urban areas, 40 to 50 percent of the children, in grade level, are reading below their levels.*

*An estimated 90 percent of the 700,000 students who drop out of school annually are classified as poor readers.*

With these statistics in the background, one is hardly startled to learn that some junior colleges are now offering remedial reading, perhaps a bit stunned that some students have reached college level but cannot read. De Anza Junior College, Cupertino, California, has reported, following tests, that 20 percent of each entering freshman class reads at a fifth-grade level or below.

. . .

Education, despite huge outlays of public money, has failed catastrophically to deal with specific mental or physical health problems, yet if we were to examine each of the estimated reading and learning-disability statistics, we would find that they are inevitably intertwined with the smaller hard-core H-LD/MBD population. Though generally of normal or high IQ, such children are entrapped at the bottom of the mushroom, along with the deaf, blind and mentally retarded.

At the same time, due to the often well-intentioned confusion of pediatrician, teacher, school administrator and parent alike, there seems to be a rush toward applying the term "learning disabled" to any child who is not performing at the expected level or who misbehaves beyond the normal. If such a diagnosis is wrong, it will leave human wreckage in its wake. Too many factors are involved. Few pediatricians or family doctors, usually through no fault of their own, are equipped by training to go much beyond an educated guess when attempting evaluation.

A number of standard and proven tests, which encompass auditory and visual coordination, speech, muscle coordination and psychological aspects, can be obtained for a reasonable fee and may be helpful in attempting to reach a preliminary decision. Frequently, however, parents of a child with evident reading difficulty will suspect eye trouble, for example, and then discover after a considerable outlay for testing that no eye defect exists.

Case histories indicate that the H-LD/MBD child can be very expensive. One family reported to me that they had spent, over a period of a relatively few years, $30,000 for tests, special schooling, psychiatric counseling and specialists of one kind or another. At the end of the heavy expenditures, conditions had not materially improved. Few families can afford such an approach and they usually must resort to endurance or to the equally unsatisfactory drug therapy programs.

H-LD/MBD knows no boundaries. Victims can be found in rich suburbia, in the homes of the middle class and in the ghettos. It cuts across all lines without regard to circumstance or ethnic group.

Even without precise statistics and taking the low estimate of one million H-LDs, American society appears to be facing a self-cycling epidemic unless it is brought under control. One leading authority, Dr. Leon Eisenberg, has stated it plainly: "I would like to suggest that some of the MBD children later present themselves as a certain subgroup of juvenile delinquents and go into later life as adults who cannot adjust normally to society." He is supported by such experts as Dr. Bernard Fox, of the National Institute of Neurological Diseases and Stroke. The Fox studies on the adult lives of untreated H-LD children indicate that they have a higher percentage of juvenile delinquency and psychiatric problems, with resultant failures in society.

A nonmedical opinion, but equally as important, was addressed to me by D. S. Akins, Provincial Probation Officer in the Ministry of Correctional Services, Ontario, Canada: "As a probation officer with many years experience, you can perhaps appreciate that I have frequently dealt with hyperkinetic children. Contacts made with educational facilities, principals and teachers, etc., when investigating for the purposes of Pre-Psychiatric Report or Social Histories, frequently reveal characteristics relating to hyperkinesis or hypersensitivity in children during their early grade school years, especially Grades 1 and 2.

"Examining school records, one frequently sees remarks

made by teachers—'could do better with more attention span—disrupts class—fidgety—will not remain in seat long enough to complete assignment.' Unfortunately, in many cases this is where the situation is left and the child's progress from grade to grade is not because of successful completion but sometimes on recommendation by teachers who want to see the last of the child. The child's problems are by-passed and he/she is labeled a 'slow learner.' We are eventually presented with a juvenile delinquent."

A convincing example came to me in a letter from a mother in Yakima, Washington: "Our son, who is now almost 20 years old, has been diagnosed as hyperkinetic. He is definitely a victim of a very short attention span, which has led to a multitude of problems in his school years with the result that he didn't get much out of schooling.

"After spending much time and money on psychiatrists, he was finally declared incorrigible by the court and spent some time in a boy's camp for problem teen-agers. After spending a year there and with no release date in sight he ran away, stole a car and is now serving time at —— Reformatory."

Another very moving letter came from a Bay Area resident: "We hyperkinetic children do become hyperkinetic adults. I should know. I am 35 years old and still suffer."

It is only logical that an affliction which may be recognized in the early months of infancy cannot be turned off automatically at the age of thirteen, seventeen or thirty-five without correcting the cause. Behavior and personality patterns undoubtedly change in many H-LD cases with the onset of puberty, but logic again dictates that there may be psychological hangovers from years of battling within and without.

# 8

# The Hazards of
# Treatment with Drugs

The use of amphetamines (stimulating drugs) to control hyperactivity began more than thirty years ago when Dr. Charles Bradley discovered that they had an opposite calming effect when administered to child patients of this syndrome. However, there is worthwhile argument by several experts that they do not really "tranquilize" at all, in a clinical sense, but simply permit concentration, which in turn lowers the level of activity.

In fact, though amphetamines are manufactured and prescribed in the millions, the exact action of these behavior-modifying drugs is not known. In fairness, the mechanisms of many healing and beneficial drugs, from aspirin to digitalis, are not known. They are often prescribed on a trial-and-error basis. If the benefits from these drugs outweigh the experiences of harm, there is no justification for abandoning them.

There was a time, however, when many doctors assumed

that if they selected the proper drug for any ailment and prescribed it to the patient in the proper dosage, healing would take place without significant harm. It is now well known that this simplistic concept is fraught with danger.

Proper dosage for a drug depends upon the patient's age, the weight (if a child), the nature and severity of the illness, as well as what other chemicals or drugs are being ingested. Yet, even with the most complete information of these factors, there will still be cases in which the accepted dosage of the drug will have an adverse effect on some individuals and be completely ineffective on others.

At present there are only two common indications where behavior-modifying drugs are prescribed to children: hyperactivity and narcolepsy (the latter is a rather rare but sometimes lifelong disorder characterized by daytime sleep patterns). Since only an occasional child is afflicted with narcolepsy, the vast majority of pediatric patients on these drugs are those considered to be H-LDs or MBDs.

Ritalin appears to be the chief drug used for treatment of hyperactivity. I encounter its use daily but I am not one of its many advocates. Total usage is somewhat difficult to determine, but Morton Mintz, medical writer for the Washington *Post*, covered aspects of the drug management in an article printed October 30, 1973:

How many children get the amphetamines and Ritalin, which CIBA-Geigy has heavily promoted for hyperkinesis, is unclear.

The number estimated in 1971 by the National Health Institute was up to 300,000. The current estimate made by CIBA-Geigy is 250,000.

A company spokesman said Friday that the firm is trying to clarify the figures in the light of testimony given at a Senate hearing in July, 1971, by CIBA-Geigy president Thomas O. Boucher.

He said that the firm in 1970 sold 243 million Ritalin tablets, that some 2 million persons took the drug, and that its use for "hyperkinesis is approaching 50 percent . . . of production." In the same year, Ritalin accounted for $11 million in sales, or 15 percent of the firm's total.

At least fifteen other drugs, in addition to Ritalin, are used in H-LD/MBD management with Dexedrine (Dextroamphetamine), said to be the second largest behavioral modifier. Ritalin, Dexedrine and Deaner (Deanol) are all classified as "central-nervous-system stimulants."

The "antianxiety and antipsychotic" compounds in use for children are Librium (Chlordiazepoxide); Thorazine (Chlorpromazine); Mellaril (Thioridazine); Atarax and Vistaril (Hydroxyzine); Prolixin and Permitil (Fluphenazine); Miltown and Equanil (Meprobamate). Tofranil (Imipramine) is used as an "antidepressant," and Dilantin (Diphenylhydantoin) as an "anticonvulsant."

The known benign "side effects" of the stimulants include nervousness, insomnia, stomach ache and skin rash. Various investigators have also reported loss of appetite leading to weight loss and increased heartbeat. No serious side effects have been attributed to Ritalin, Dexedrine or Deaner.

Effects of a more serious nature have been reported for most of the antianxiety drugs. They include jaundice and leukopenia, a decrease in the number of white cells in the child's blood. Benign effects of these drugs include drowsiness, dizziness and nasal congestion.

The largest single dosage of Ritalin that I have encountered is 125 mgm, administered at 7 A.M., at noon and at

7 P.M. I was staggered, though, when I heard of a single dosage of 100 mgm of Mellaril administered to one child before bedtime. However the child fared, I don't know how the doctor managed to close his eyes at night.

Perhaps because there have been only a limited number of studies, there is no hard evidence that these drugs will lead to addiction. However, there is certainly ample evidence that they can become psychological crutches. Logic plus medical experience compel me to believe that no patient, particularly no child, can be drug-managed for eight years or more, beginning at the age of three or four, without risk.

One boy, whom I shall call Johnny Ten, which was his age, was very frightened when he came into the office. He became even more frightened when I told his mother, in his presence, that I planned to take him off drugs within a month. When I asked him why he was frightened, he replied, "When I don't have the pills, I feel like I'll explode inside."

The youngster had been on Ritalin for two years. Within three weeks after he started the K-P Diet, he was off drugs, and the "explosive" feeling departed. Subsequent checks revealed no psychological problems as a result of stopping drug therapy.

Dr. J. Gordon Millichap, of the Departments of Neurology and Pediatrics, Northwestern University Medical School and Children's Memorial Hospital, Chicago, studied "Drugs in Management of Minimal Brain Dysfunction" and presented his findings at an MBD symposium in New York in 1973. They later appeared in the *Annals of the New York Academy of Sciences*.

Dr. Millichap wrote: "It is the consensus among physicians that there is a place for central nervous system stimulants in the treatment of hyperkinetic behavioral disorders in children. These medications should be prescribed with suitable controls, under proper medical supervision and as adjuncts to remedial education."

Summarizing, Millichap stated that "The ideal drug for the treatment of children with MBD should control hyperactivity, increase attention span, reduce impulsive and aggressive behavior, and have measurable beneficial effects on visual and auditory perception, reading ability, and coordination, without inducing insomnia, anorexia, drowsiness or other, more serious toxic effects."

That is a large order for any drug, and it seems to me, the "ideal" may be unattainable. Millichap, on the other hand, concluded that Ritalin and Dexedrine were justified and recommended several of the antianxiety or antidepressant drugs as alternatives.

Yet the camp is very much divided. As an antidrug physician, *in this particular case*, I believe these medications should be used only as a last resort when everything else—certainly including diet—has been tried and has failed. Far too often, drugs are prescribed as a first measure.

Not one drug listed by the Millichap study is without its side effects, benign or serious. Additionally, the psychological effects of long-term usage, which may or may not lead to some form of addiction, are still in gray areas.

Another aspect was raised in a study by Drs. L. Alan Sroufe and Mark A. Stewart. Discussing drug therapy in junior high school and high school, Stewart cited cases where "extra pills were taken before tests." Sale of drugs was also involved in cases at this grade level.

Additional caution in the use of Dextroamphetamine management for the hyperactive child was indicated in the February 1974 issue of the *Western Journal of Medicine* with a report by Drs. Lawrence M. Greenburg, University of California, at Davis, School of Medicine; Shirley McMahon, pediatrician of Marblehead, Massachusetts; and Michael A. Deem, research associate at Children's Hospital, Washington, D.C.

In subjecting twenty-six H-LD children to a "double blind, placebo-controlled, short-term comparative study of the effects of Dextroamphetamine and two other medications," they found that five patients reacted with symptoms of "disorganization" and "depression." Even manic tendencies were noted. The symptoms abated or disappeared after cessation of the amphetamines.

Most of the drug upheaval occurred after World War II, and drug abuses by young people in the late sixties were primarily responsible for the Food and Drug Administration's decision in 1970 to restrict amphetamines in regard to children. Japan banned amphetamines long ago, England restricted their usage to hospital pharmacies in 1968, and Sweden had categorized them as narcotics as early as 1944. Yet the estimated production of amphetamine-type drugs in the United States in 1971 was 8 billion tablets. Aside from the profit motive, the need for that many tablets is questionable.

In 1972 the FDA sliced the production of Ritalin in half and also placed the drug, and certain amphetamine types, on the Schedule II list—the same category as opium, codeine and morphine. This action illustrated the true nature of the stimulant drugs.

It was not until 1958 that Dr. Leon Eisenberg, then at Johns Hopkins University, now at Harvard, had begun to delve into the comparatively unknown territory of evaluating stimulant drugs for behavioral problems of children. The

work was carried on under a grant from the National In-
titute of Mental Health.

There had been earlier research, dating back to the thirties and forties, but it lacked in technique. Eisenberg's work,
followed by that of Dr. C. Keith Conners and others,
erected danger flags on the indiscriminate use of amphetamines in the treatment of H-LDs. After more than ten years
of testing and study, the consensus of many investigators
involved in this work is that the drugs have a short-term
effect at best, and might be creating as many problems as
they appear to solve.

Despite the findings and cautions of experienced investigators, which continue to appear in medical publications,
a number of physicians dispense the behavior-modifying
drugs freely, on many occasions apparently without any
degree of certainty that they are dealing with a true H-LD.

To make matters worse, doctors subscribing wholeheartedly to this drug therapy are often abetted by educators
who find medication the simplest route to classroom quiet.
The victim of both points of view is the hapless H-LD/MBD.

In some states, children on this type of medication must
be identified in school records. California Education Code
12020 (AB 1501) requires that school personnel be notified
if a child is on continuing medication. The identification,
placed in school records, is likely to follow the child through
college, perhaps years after the problem is solved, or at least
contained. Parents have told me that it is almost impossible
to eradicate the information from records.

Viewed totally, drug management of the H-LD appears
to have more in the minus column than in the plus. Therefore, in my opinion, it is doubtful therapy and should be
last-resort therapy.

In another one of those medical surprises, I remember

my own uneasy puzzlement when I arrived at the conclusion that the dye in the very drug that was supposed to be helping one H-LD might be the cause of a reverse effect. In this case, we had put a boy on the elimination diet and his medication was being phased out. Then, when his mother finally cut down the drug dosage to half a tablet a day, it seemed to have a stimulating effect on him, exactly the opposite of some two years of experience with it.

Troubled, I spilled one of the blue 10-mgm tablets onto the top of my desk, broke it in half and studied it for a moment. I had no idea what minuscule amount of dye was contained in it, but I could find no other reason for the rapid change. I called the boy's mother and told her to stop medication, to let the diet try to compensate for the lack of stimulant.

The procedure worked, an indication that the reduction of the dosage was not causing the countereffect. Cessation of the drug, combined with elimination of the food synthetics, brought about the sought-after calming effect.

# 9

# Success and Failure
# with the Diet

There have been other surprises in the K-P Diet management. A child at the Northern Montana Mental Retardation Center displayed all the patterns of hyperkinesis. At the same time, he was a PKU (phenylketonuria), an inherited abnormal condition caused by faulty metabolism of phenylalanine, an amino acid essential to the nutrition of man and animal alike.

The disease shows up early, usually in forms of mental retardation. Clearly mentally disturbed, this particular child was also increasingly disruptive and aggressive in many ways. Frustrated easily, he would flare out against others or turn wrath inward by biting himself. Punishment meant nothing. He was on the verge of being "unmanageable," according to his immediate supervisor. Fifty milligrams of Thorazine had been prescribed as a control.

Yet hyperkinesis is not usually associated with PKU. The supervisor, searching for a method of added control, learned of the elimination diet and wondered if certain foods might not be stirring up the patient. The boy ate the same institutional foods as the other children, but experimentally, the staff member eliminated all synthetics and all natural salicylates from his diet. Within three weeks, most of the hyperkinetic symptoms had disappeared. The unrelated PKU condition was not influenced.

Although I am convinced that adverse reactions to food additives are nonimmunologic, allergy occasionally appears to be involved in H-LD cases. Through heredity, 20 to 25 percent of the human race have a tendency to be allergic. On this basis, twenty to twenty-five out of every hundred H-LD/MBD children are likely subjects for allergic reactions which are usually totally independent of their behavioral disturbance.

Allergy can be likened to a volcano, remaining completely dormant for variable periods, or it may steam and sputter intermittently or persistently. In a similar manner, an individual may have an allergic state which is inactive. For various reasons, symptoms of allergy may suddenly develop. Like the volcano, these may be mild or severe and intermittent or persistent. At times the volcano can react violently, emitting molten lava with clouds of steam and flames. Similarly, a quiescent or mild allergic state may become very active and manifest itself as severe hives, eczema or asthma, and the reaction may be severe enough to cause shock and even death.

In dealing with the H-LD who is also allergic, I have found that approximately 50 percent will respond to the K-P Diet without any special attention paid to the allergy. However, with a very small percentage, when allergy is present, management for the allergy must be instituted in order for the diet to succeed.

69

A three-and-a-half-year-old girl was on the elimination diet for forty-nine days but failed to show an improvement in her behavior. Upon skin testing, it was demonstrated that the child was sensitive to jute fiber and cattle hair, both of which are used in the manufacture of felt carpet padding. The family had felt carpet padding in the home. Following its removal the child responded quickly to the elimination diet with a pronounced improvement in her behavior.

I have made the same observation following the removal from the home of other environmental factors, such as feather pillows, and furry pets like dogs and cats.

A young male hyperkinetic failed to respond to the elimination diet. From his history of milk intolerance in early infancy, a sensitivity to milk was suspected. Following the elimination of milk, in addition to the K-P Diet, an immediate improvement was noted in the boy's behavior.

In rare cases, allergy appears to be a prime factor in causing the hyperactive disturbance. Food synthetics are not involved. A good response may be observed, following management of the allergy. The role that allergy plays in any child can only be determined by trial and error.

As an overall guide it is important to know that the effect of allergy (with or without observable symptoms) upon the behavioral pattern is the opposite of that seen with hyperkinesis. The allergic children complain of fatigue, listlessness and lassitude. They are not active. In addition, they have a pale, wan expression with dark circles under the eyes, a fish-shaped pursing of the lips and a crease over the tip of the nose. The combined pattern is commonly referred to as the "tension-fatigue" syndrome and indicates allergy.

Along with the successes, there have been partial to complete failures to respond to the K-P Diet. Out of my first twenty-five patients, eight did not respond. The same ratio, more or less, has continued as experience broadens. The best estimate, based on careful records, is that 50 percent have a likelihood of full response, while 75 percent can be removed from drug management, even if full response to other symptoms is not achieved. That result alone would appear to make trial a worthy venture.

In Judith Keithley's first group of hyperkinetics, including the enchanting "Billy" and his "withdrawal" problems, eleven out of thirteen children achieved full response. But a second Keithley group of twenty H-LDs fell to a 50 percent full-response achievement, supporting the diet performance of those children that I have personally managed. Hoping to again reach a 70 to 80 percent mark, Keithley was dismayed at the failure rate. However, many factors are involved.

Some failures are rather easy to assess. A few parents did not adhere strictly to the diet, or the children flatly refused to cooperate. Others, of course, tried it, and were frank to say it was "too much nuisance and bother," no fault of the diet itself. I discovered that some children were influenced by others during school periods. They were urged to eat candy or consume soft drinks. It is very difficult for the H-LD to resist peer pressure.

The balance of the failures did not respond, for unknown reasons. There are the previously mentioned possibilities to consider: actual undiagnosed brain damage from birth difficulties; toxemia suffered by mother during pregnancy; other unidentified disorders.

Perhaps one or two of the eight failures in my own group of twenty-five hyperkinetics were not being "turned on" by food flavors and colors. Further and lengthy investigation of all the failures might provide answers of an entirely different nature.

However, I'm inclined to think that if 50 percent, even 25 percent, of the H-LDs will respond to inexpensive dietary management, it is well worth the family's effort. If the children of this particular group—those apparently reacting to food additives—can be taken off drug therapy and permitted to lead normal lives at home and in school, enabling enough concentration to climb out of the "learning-disability" trap, the admitted bother and kitchen nuisance becomes both productive and rewarding.

It is easy to understand the problems of the parents, beyond the nuisance factor, in skirting the possible "turn-ons" in the food supply. One mother with two small H-LD-problem males (an unusual occurrence within one family) reported complete failure, but her diet diary revealed a steady intake of commercial doughnuts, pretzels and bacon.

Another mother reported: "We have not noticed a dramatic change in his behavior. The teacher does not notice a marked difference. There is an indication that he is more receptive to doing what he is asked to do. He may be sitting still for a longer period of time."

I requested a copy of her diary. There were seventeen infractions over a fourteen-day period. They included processed ice cream, pancakes, waffles, sweet rolls, chocolates, salami, carob bar and chocolate milk.

Patient refusal is another aspect. One entire family was being disrupted by an eight-year-old. They were seeing a social worker twice a week; the boy visited a psychologist twice monthly. The social worker attempted to persuade the family to try the diet. She informed me later, "His parents thought it was too much for them to follow." The final decision was made by the eight-year-old. He simply refused it. The diet management cannot succeed if parental management is weak or wavering. Firmness mixed with understanding is the answer. In addition, it is important to recognize that many of these children are not able to make decisions for themselves. Their impulsive behavior is beyond their control.

Beyond diet infractions contributing to the failures, it is conceivable that other chemicals, about which we know very little or nothing, are involved in some patients— preservatives, possibly, or naturally occurring chemicals. It is possible that certain foods are delivering natural trace elements—heavy metals—triggering responses in a Y group, yet not affecting an X group. Man is still in the dark as to what exact role the trace elements play in the human system. Environmental pollution involving some of the metals cannot be ruled out. Time and further research may shed light.

The majority of children that are true H-LDs and under constant drug management seem to be willing to do almost anything to get "off the pills." I remember one plump blond boy of ten who was in a disability class, sedated with a daily dosage of 100 mgm of Dilantin. Today he's in a class for gifted children. He does the afternoon shopping for his divorced and working mother, taking the diet list with him when he patrols the supermarket aisles. I think he's heroic.

There are many incentives. One nine-year-old boy had always wanted to build model airplanes but couldn't sit still long enough; his hands couldn't perform the intricate work of fitting struts, putting the tiny parts into place. His incentive to stay strictly on the diet was the building of miniatures. Several have now been completed.

73

Another boy knew that he was scholastically capable, brighter than most of the other children in his class. Yet he always wound up at the tail end. His incentive against temptation at the candy rack was to get out of the cellar. He's now an honor student.

*Most of the children don't want to be bad. They don't want to be on drugs. They don't want to be in learning-disability classes. They are not subintelligent. In my opinion, they are chemically abused. These children are normal. Their environment is abnormal.*

And most of those whom I have personally observed are willing to make sacrifices if their parents and teachers will join them. While the average child will break the rules, at home and away from home, particularly with candy, the parents must attempt to police them closely in the first ten days or two weeks, a period usually long enough to break the cycle and quiet them down. Then management is simpler.

When parents say the child is on the diet "70 to 80 percent," it means he can recycle himself. A candy bar on Monday sets off a pattern that can last to Wednesday or even Thursday. If he has a Popsicle or fruit punch that day, it may carom in his system for the rest of the week.

The chemical "turn-ons" can also work like a slowly building storm, breaking suddenly. A thirteen-year-old newspaper carrier, on Ritalin and Desoxyn management, won a subscription contest to Kansas City and came home a wreck. For four days he struggled through one emotional crisis after another. It was much more than the usual reaction to exhaustion and excitement. His parents questioned him and learned that he'd ingested little but hot dogs, soft drinks and ice cream, the usual "away from home" treats

74

for a fun outing of this sort. The other boys apparently suffered no ill effects, but the intake for this H-LD resulted in a four-day tailspin.

Except for the first two or three weeks of dietary management, when it is important to break the usual diet cycle, no older child can be, nor should he be, monitored constantly. The young child, however, must be watched closely. Away from home, whether on a long trip, at school, or just across the street in a neighbor's kitchen, the degree of cooperation has to depend on the child, and on how much he or she wants to "kick" the emotional outbursts and medication. Excessive measures are not likely to work.

One mother asked, "Why can't I put a lock on the refrigerator?"

I answered, "And maybe add a psychological problem? Don't lock it. Just take the junk out of it."

Further, experience has shown that the entire situation will be improved if the parents do not endlessly discuss the diet and the problem with the child or with other family members.

One father was analyzing the progress, making a big thing of the diet. The subject came up at most meals—often an explosive period for the H-LD, anyway. The young patient realized that *he* was the sole reason the whole family was on food control. I said to the father, "Stop it! Get off the subject. Let it run its course."

The child was improving. Except for more planning and extra kitchen time, the meal situation had not changed radically. The family was eating all meats, seafood and poultry. Only luncheon meats, some bacon, frankfurters and some sausages had been banned. Fresh vegetables and greens were plentiful on the table. They now had homemade pastries, which were as good or better than those purchased at the store. The health of the entire family could improve sans the synthetics.

"Why even discuss it?" I asked. "Eat heartily."

*The entire family should go on the diet.* The H-LD should not be singled out to eat his "special" food while all others dive into favorites he can't tolerate. Older children not burdened with hyperkinesis can snack away, if they choose, off the premises. Quite simply, it is a matter of being fair, of sharing a common goal.

Once firm diagnosis is made, best results are obtained if management is started early. The child of five or six actually appears to make an easier adjustment than the older child. The teen-ager may rebel entirely.

Although the elimination diet is rigid in regard to synthetic chemical flavors and colors, there is ample flexibility to experiment, as time goes by, and attempt various foods with a natural salicylate radical. If there is no history of aspirin-sensitivity in either parent, the diet may be cautiously expanded.

Tomatoes can be tried, then some of the fruits. Perhaps the patient will tolerate peaches or apricots, cucumbers or fresh orange juice. The mother will soon be able to judge what foods are safe.

If the diet diary shows many infractions and the child is still doing well, it would be reasonable to assume that *chemical factors are not involved*. The child doesn't fit into the pattern of this particular group of H-LDs. The synthetics can then be eliminated as a causative factor, which may be just as important a result. Other causes must be investigated, particularly whether or not the child is a true H-LD.

# 10

## The Problem of
## Food Labeling

With seven of her eleven primary students reliably diagnosed as H-LDs, a teacher in a Brooklyn school for handicapped children decided to analyze the ingredients of the school's "good breakfast" program. By current standards, there was nothing especially wrong with the nutritional balance, but she discovered that 80 percent of the foods for the daily starting meal were synthetically colored and flavored, a figure which would likely not vary too much in similar "good breakfast" situations throughout the country.

The all-important morning meal for the H-LDs, and for all children, often has the highest daily ratio, per meal, of the synthetics. One possible reason is that breakfast, at home or in school, is usually the most hurried meal of the day in terms of preparation.

The customary fruit juice is usually canned, frozen concentrate or otherwise, with the housewife-mother having a wide variety of flavors from which to choose. She can range from citrus to exotic South Seas–type drinks. But many of the fruit juices or so-called "punches" in the jumbo-sized cans are almost totally synthetic, aside from water content.

With oatmeal, cornflakes and bran flakes now apparently considered old-fashioned, the American cereals for juniors often come in gaily decorated boxes with a kaleidoscope of colors inside, matching the lithography on the outside. They run a phantasmagoric gamut from bright yellow and red to purple and pink, a rainbow parade of kernels undeniably attractive to young eyes. They are given names to excite children. Then the result of the persuasion shows up in the grocery cart.

Breakfast cereals with chemical flavors are available from chocolate taste to almost every berry and fruit mentionable. For super-quick service there are the "instant breakfasts" with intimations that they are equally nutritious for children. Mixed into almost all of them are other additives for "better shelf life" and sundry purposes.

Occasionally I've wondered whether or not the board chairmen and presidents of certain giant companies really know what is in their products. Perhaps they don't have children or grandchildren. Perhaps they have tunnel vision focused on sales charts. Perhaps they don't care.

In 1970 Robert B. Choate, of the Council on Children, Media and Advertising, appearing before a Senate subcommittee, declared that the "most nutritional part of cereal is the box." Allowing for warranted sarcasm, I chuckled, but hollowly. Since Choate's testimony it has been reported that thirty-six of the forty cereals under fire have been upgraded nutritionally. It is dismaying that it took public pressure to force the cereal makers to live up to advertising claims.

An estimated $400 million is spent annually on television commercials directed toward the "kiddie market," and much emphasis is on the sweet tooth. The built-in weakness of all children is exploited. Some cereals have more sugar than grain content.

The companies involved are not backyard operations. They are mammoth, and reek of respectability. When attacked, they appear to be stunned, as if their products were made in heaven. I find it hard to believe that they are not aware of the dangers of high sugar content; or that the paint pot of colors inside many boxes is of absolutely no benefit and of possible harm. (If nothing else, they are needless.)

Breakfast over, if the child buys lunch at school, particularly at the snack bar, the additives will be revisited. The school nutritionist has little choice but to buy from the common American food supply. In doing so, the additives of all varieties are inescapable.

The H-LD, as separated from the individuals who are not "turned on," is being bombed from breakfast forward, in my findings. Most of the sample menus that parents of H-LD children have submitted vary from 25 to 50 percent in usage of foods that are artificially flavored and colored. The same items keep bobbing up: the same brands of dry cereals, and hot dogs, cakes, cookies, ice cream, Popsicles, fruit punches, soft drinks, quick-mix powdered drinks.

The menus may or may not be representative of what the average American child ingests, but I'm inclined to think they are good indicators for a considerable segment of the population. Reviewing them, I become doubly aware of the synthetic penetration of the food supply and of the kitchen and menu-planning difficulties. For instance, one seldom thinks of synthetics in relation to cheese, margarine

79

and chocolate milk. Yet most brands of all three products have coloring, if not flavoring. (White cheese escapes the color, of course.) Many luncheon meats are doctored with additives. Most packaged seasonings and soup mixes have synthetic residents.

The salicylates pose an added problem. Fresh orange juice has a salicylate radical, as do cucumbers (automatically eliminating pickles). Cider vinegar has a salicylate from apples; wine vinegar's salicylate comes from grapes. (White distilled vinegar has no salicylate.) The frozen-concentrate and canned orange juices have a salicylate radical plus the likelihood of synthetics; the fruit punches are also likely to contain a salicylate, with other synthetics a certainty. Even wholesome apple juice and prune juice become casualties due to their chemical structure.

It would indeed be a bleak breakfast-juice future for the H-LD and the menu planner if grapefruit, grapefruit juice and pineapple juice did not come to the rescue. Nature skipped these fruits, among others, when allocating salicylates.

Condiments are also a problem. Ketchup, made from tomatoes, has a salicylate, and some brands add a dab of synthetic flavoring. Chili sauce is in the same category. Several brands of mustard lean heavily on synthetics. Most brands of mayonnaise now depend on synthetics, although one national brand declares itself free of the chemical additives. Fortunately, this indispensable dressing is quite simple to make at home.

The average mother of a hyperactive child dutifully provides the daily table without really thinking too much about ingredients. The following six-day chart, covering a period in August 1973 from a Sunday to the following Friday, is rather typical of the H-LD sample menus, prior to diet management, for the hot summer months. I have italicized the known "additive foods," limiting my guess to the probability of artificial flavoring and coloring, and natural salicylates:

## SUNDAY

BREAKFAST
*Orange juice*
Scrambled egg—1 egg with milk
1 slice toast with corn oil *margarine*
*Blackberry jelly*
Glass *ice tea* (tea contains a salicylate)

LUNCHEON
Slice of *bologna* and baked ham
Small slice of *pepperoni cheese*
Small slice of *cheddar cheese*
*Cherry Kool-Aid*
3 store cookies—*raspberry jelly*; *coconut*
and *marshmallow.*
*2 plums*; *1 peach*
*1 candy peppermint*
Peanuts

DINNER
Beef roast
Potatoes cooked with roast
Gravy made with cornstarch
Wax beans with *margarine*
Tossed salad—lettuce, celery, green pepper, *tomato* (dressing, Wesson Oil, *vinegar* and *sweet pickle juice*)
Bananas sprinkled with dry *cherry Jell-O*
*Peppermint patty, cherry Popsicle, orange Popsicle*

## MONDAY

BREAKFAST  Bowl of Wheaties with milk and sugar
½ English muffin with *margarine*
*Orange juice*
*Orange Popsicle*

LUNCHEON  *Vegetable beef soup*
*Lemon-Lime Kool-Aid*
*Vanilla ice cream with chocolate sauce*

DINNER  Hamburger with *catsup, mustard,* lettuce
and onion
Potatoes fried in Wesson Oil
*Vanilla ice cream with chocolate sauce*
*Chocolate milk*

SNACKS  *Sweet pickle, bologna,* potato chips, Swiss
cheese
*Kool-Aid*
Cup of granola, with milk and sugar
½ pear

## TUESDAY

BREAKFAST  *Orange juice*
French toast with *margarine, syrup* and
powdered sugar

LUNCHEON  Hamburger on bread with *catsup, mustard, pickle* and *tomato*
Potato chips
*Kool-Aid*
*Vanilla and chocolate sandwich cookies*
Peanuts

DINNER    Beef stew made with beef, potatoes, car-
rots, celery and onions
Garlic bread (store)
*Vanilla and chocolate sandwich cookies*
*Chocolate milk*
Tossed salad with *bottled dressing*
*2 grape Popsicles*

---

## WEDNESDAY

BREAKFAST   *Orange juice*
*Boo Berry cereal* with milk

LUNCHEON   *Bologna and salami*
*Grape pop*
Peanuts

DINNER    Macaroni and *cheese—cheese sauce* made
from *cheddar cheese soup*
Coleslaw
French fries
*Chocolate ice cream*
*Chocolate milk*

---

## THURSDAY

BREAKFAST   *Orange juice*
*Boo Berry cereal* with milk

LUNCHEON   Sandwich—1 slice of bread with *bologna,
chicken loaf* and *cheese*
Potato chips
*Kool-Aid*

*Popsicle*
*2 caramel candies*

DINNER      Salisbury steak with onion gravy—*Lipton soup mix*
Noodles
Tossed salad with *bottled dressing*
*Popsicle*
*4 pieces of candy*

---

**FRIDAY**

BREAKFAST      *Orange juice*
*Boo Berry cereal* with milk

LUNCHEON      Macaroni and *cheese*
Coleslaw
*Chocolate ice cream*
*Kool-Aid*

SNACKS      *Chocolate and vanilla sandwich cookies*
Potato chips
*Kool-Aid*

DINNER      Spaghetti and meat balls—sauce made from *packaged seasoning*
Tossed salad
Bread
*Chocolate milk*
*Ice cream*
*Piece of candy*

An expert in additives may find that I've missed several items that are usually artificially doctored for hue and taste. But moving through the sample menus or scanning along the shelves to avoid the additives is similar to skipping across a culinary minefield.

One mother said, "I find *she* could die of starvation if I exclude all artificial flavorings and colorings." This is not very likely (see the menus at the end of the book), but I well appreciate the formidable and frustrating kitchen task of planning menus for the K-P Diet. Reading food labels may become a modern art, but even the masters will fail on occasion.

Some flavors must be listed by FDA regulation. Others seem to escape labeling, either by processor's design or legal loophole. One of the top brands of soup simply lists "flavoring" in its descriptions of ingredients and leaves the customer to guess whether it is synthetic or natural. It is not required to disclose contents of cheese, butter and ice cream, though some manufacturers volunteer the information.

The coloring is usually mentioned but often appears as "artificial color" or "U.S. Certified," without the type designated. A top brand of "imitation margarine" lists its color as "carotene" but fails to name its artificial flavoring. A top brand of cheese reports that it is "artificially colored" but avoids naming that notorious yellow chemical. An instant chocolate, also a best seller, lists "vanillin" and "other" artificial flavorings.

Strange are the ways of labeling. MSG, or monosodium glutamate, is a seaweed or soybean flavor enhancer, not a flavor, borrowed from the Orient but synthesized differently in the United States, and is present in thousands of products. For reasons known only to the government, it must appear on labels when used in soups and canned goods, but this requirement does not apply to salad dressings or mayonnaise. However, all these foods head for a common gathering ground—the stomach.

Once added to many baby foods, MSG was voluntarily withdrawn from most infant products when it appeared to damage the brains of newborn offspring of several species of animals. A substitute, hydrolized vegetable protein, also called protein hydrolysate, in which the amino acids are released in free form, has taken its place in some jars and cans. This substance is widely used in all types of food and is presumably safe.

Beyond the confusion in regulations concerning specific ingredients, there is often a ballet of words as manufacturers dance around the facts in the "main title" of the product. *Chicken Flavored Soup* is apt to mean that no chicken was ever near the broth, and the H-LD mother would be advised to scan the label closely; only the flavor made contact. *Chicken Soup* usually means that at least a little of the bird managed to find its way to the vat.

In January 1973 the FDA announced a twelve-part program to "provide the American consumer with specific and meaningful new information on the identity, quality and nutritional value of a wide variety of general and special foods available in the nation's marketplace."

Charles C. Edwards, M.D., former commissioner of Food and Drugs, said it was the "beginning of a new era in providing consumers with complete, concise and informative food labeling."

As an example of the change: "If the vanilla pudding contains no artificial flavor, it would be called 'vanilla pudding.' If it contains a natural flavor which predominates, with an added artificial flavor, it would be then called 'vanilla flavored pudding.' If both natural and artificial flavorings are used, and the artificial flavoring predominates, the name would be 'artificially flavored vanilla pudding.' If only artificial flavor is used, it would also be 'artificially flavored vanilla pudding.' "

So much for pudding regulations, but it might be hoped the H-LD mother will also learn that "vanillin" on the label means a synthetic, while "vanilla" is the pure, good ingredient. Natural vanilla is now designated by the "Vanillamark," a new symbol. Caught without glasses or standing in a shadowy corner, the shopper just might be confused. The K-P Diet overseer will still need a sharp eye and mind to guide him through the phraseology.

The manufacturers do have some options as the result of past handling of Section 401, Federal Food, Drug and Cosmetic Act. I have read the four different categories several times. Lacking expertise, I cannot interpret the quartet. Yet I come to the conclusion that they offer some loopholes:

*Mandatory Ingredients* (some of which do not have to be labeled); *Permissible Mandatory Ingredients* (some of which do not have to be labeled); *Unlabeled Optional Ingredients* (which do not have to be labeled); *Labeled Optional Ingredients* (some of which do not have to be labeled).

Currently the FDA is *not authorized* to require a complete ingredient statement for foods covered by current standards, but the agency has strongly urged that such information be provided by processors and has requested Congress to pass legislation granting the necessary authority.

To be of benefit to H-LD parents, such legislation would have to include the following requirements:

1. Disclosure should be complete, detailed and specific— in other words, not the current practice of stipulating artificial color and flavor as simply "flavor" and "color" without precise specifications. Adding "raspberry" or "FD & C Red 2" would not overly burden a label but would permit a

physician to target a possible specific irritant. The benefits would go far beyond the H-LD situation.

2. Ingredients should be displayed prominently on the label and not in an obscure or unreadable location, such as the bleed-off into a bottle-cap crimp. One should not have to acquire 3-D vision to read labels.

3. Disclosures should be in a typeface that is legible to the average eye.

4. Labeling should not be misleading: large type specifying "no artificial preservatives," while hidden in fine print is "artificial color and flavor." The average consumer reads the truthful "no artificial preservatives" and often takes for granted that no other synthetics are in the product.

One possible solution might be a symbol, or symbols, which would signify that no synthetic colors or flavors are present in the product. Whether government- or industry-originated, such identification would quickly remove doubts.

Pressure to weaken regulations is always present. Some years ago the coloring industry felt uncomfortable with the designation "coal-tar colors" because of consumer association with the black, sticky basic product. The industry managed to have the government delete the "coal tar" wording on grounds that the final product was refined many times and bore no resemblance to the product of origin. Now some portions of the additive industry are apparently uncomfortable with the term "imitation."

The same White House Conference on Food, Nutrition and Health that proposed the twelve-part regulation changes also recommended that "oversimplified and inaccurate terms such as 'imitation' should be abandoned as uninformative to the public."*

The conference then proposed to "set up a mechanism

* Health, Education & Welfare News Release 73-2.

so that a product which is similar to an established food product, and at least nutritionally equivalent to that product, could be marketed without the use of the word 'imitation.' "

This "mechanism" would appear to be serving up industry options on a very wide platter. For those unlucky members of the public who are sensitive to certain chemicals, the word "imitation" is far from uninformative. It means that the product is likely to be liberally penetrated with synthetics. The mother of an H-LD would have no protection against that particular item.

Preparing for a symposium on additives in the late 1960s, I wrote to the president of one of America's leading food-processing companies requesting a list of flavorings and colorings used in their products, particularly in dry cereals. In time, the company's chief nutritionist replied that they only used "certified" additives and that I could obtain further information from the FDA.

I directed another letter to the president of this internationally known company, a Midwest giant, and again the chief nutritionist answered, calling attention to her previous reply. In answering this second useless letter, I said I was sorry I couldn't get their cooperation and that they left me no alternative but to recommend, at the symposium, that their products not be used. A copy was forwarded to the company head.

Within two days I received an apologetic long-distance call and assurances that the full information would be mailed within a short time. It soon arrived, but I found myself wondering about its reliability, despite the company's supposedly impeccable reputation. Perhaps the list was fully accurate, but the initial tactics of evasion naturally made me suspicious.

Another encounter with a large retail food chain in San Francisco was almost a replay of this experience. When a new beef product was introduced I called the chief butcher to ask, "Do you have artificial flavoring and coloring in that?"

"No coloring, but we have flavoring," he answered. He could not identify the flavoring.

A few days later I went into one of the chain's cavernous supermarts and found the new product in the meat case. It lacked a label of contents but was branded with the trade name. I asked the butcher on duty about the label. "Well, they made a mistake," he said and added that he'd just received a memo saying the product would soon be properly labeled.

About two weeks later I went back to the same store; the product now bore a label of contents, without mention of flavor. I called the office of the chain's president and was promptly referred to the public relations director, who said he would investigate. Soon I received a letter stating that the product was not artificially flavored but contained a "hydrolized protein." Was I to believe the PR man or the chief butcher?

Both incidents are examples of the great difficulty in obtaining accurate information on the contents of processed foods. If a medical doctor cannot easily persuade industry to divulge what should be shared knowledge for the benefit of health, the general public has small chance of success.

My instructions to parents of H-LDs on the K-P Diet are: "If you look at the label and you're suspicious, don't use the product. One mouthful can upset the child."

But no matter how suspicious, no matter if labels are analyzed with a magnifying glass, the parent cannot be adequately prepared for the hidden carriers. For instance, I would never think of placing turkey on the elimination list, yet the new self-basters contain artificial flavoring and coloring. When heat is applied, the basting material diffuses throughout the turkey—and with it, the synthetics.

# 11

# The Problem of Medications for Children

Medicating the H-LD who is disturbed by synthetic additives also requires considerable thought and effort.

Example: A hyperkinetic child of five has a pesky common cold, characterized by the usual runny nose, slight fever and moderate hacking cough. The mother knows she cannot administer the pink baby aspirin because it is artificially colored. She cannot even crush a half tablet of the nonflavored, noncolored adult aspirin because there may be a salicylate reaction.

She goes to the druggist and requests a cough syrup that does not contain flavoring or coloring (to my knowledge, there are none). Probably, since she has tried to obtain the item previously, she anticipates a negative reply. So she is forced to take home a synthetic fruit-flavored concoction, often colored red, and the misery of the cold is soon complicated by other reactions.

If the same child develops a severe upper-respiratory illness, the physician also finds himself at a loss to prescribe medications that are free of the additives. Most antibiotics, bronchodilators and decongestants for child patients have the palatable, synthetic ingredients.

But the problem is not limited to pediatrics. Adult patients who react adversely to the medication additives face an almost identical dilemma, which taxes the ingenuity of the doctors to find suitable medicines that will not backfire.

The role of pediatric medications in the H-LD is not known but is being studied. One child, in a case reported to me, was diagnosed as arthritic at the age of three and placed on infant-aspirin management with a dosage of twenty-seven tablets a day, a considerable dosage. At age five the child was judged to be nonarthritic by another physician, and the aspirin management was stopped. By this time the child was also hyperkinetic. Was the aspirin at fault? There is no way to prove it, and it cannot be blamed. Yet it can't be eliminated as a possibility.

Modern pharmacology has all but conquered the bitter doses of the previous centuries. The patient is now pretty well conditioned from infancy to want and expect medication that doesn't look or taste like medication. Pampering or not, it is a good idea that is psychologically beneficial.

Medications for children, particularly for infants, should be as pleasing as possible. A medicine that is partially or wholly rejected by an infant, because of foul taste, cannot do its job—the precise and excellent reason for the additives.

However, in solving the medication taste-look problem with the synthetics for the broad mass of patients, pharmacy also inherits the smaller group of individuals who cannot tolerate the additives. The obvious answer is to create a line of drugs, particularly for pediatric practice, that is free of the artificials, or a line flavored with honey or another natural syrup.

Yet, it is not quite that simple! In early spring 1973, after the mother of an ill H-LD frantically sought to obtain additive-free prescriptions, I wrote to one of the largest pharmaceutical companies in the country to request its leadership in instituting a line of such products. I believed that if this prestigious firm would pathfind the program, others would follow.

The medical director of the company was sympathetic but doubtful: "The difficulties in medicating patients who have allergies to artificial colors and flavors can easily be appreciated. For the older child and the adult the answer is probably not too difficult; the use of tablet forms which, although not containing coloring or flavoring, do contain other excipients. However, I would imagine that most manufacturers will let you have information about the inactive ingredients in their products.

"Where a liquid preparation is needed, however, I can see real problems. The major problem from the manufacturer's point of view is that the elimination of coloring and/or flavoring can make an NDA [New Drug Application] out of an old product. The FDA would demand bioavailability data from the two preparations before they would be willing to allow commercial release of the non-flavored and non-colored preparation. Frankly, I doubt that most manufacturers would be willing or could spare the effort and facilities for such a process. However, I think this is basically a marketing type of decision and I shall certainly bring your suggestion to the Marketing Department of our organization."

I appreciated his candor but believed the problem demanded greater interest than the marketing department of any pharmaceutical house.

FDA regulations wisely demand that any change in product be supported by extensive testing. In this case, specific rules regarding the colors and flavors, although they are classified as *inert ingredients*, would send the already approved product back to the labs for perhaps years of tests.

While wholeheartedly supporting all current tests and advocating an even wider range of testing, I could not understand the logic of the FDA forcing complete "new product" evaluation on an approved product, simply because of the elimination of, in some cases, potentially harmful ingredients. They were already admittedly "cosmetic" and of no healing value.

Unfortunately, it appears that the medical director of the drug company was correct. The FDA substantially confirmed that manufacturers would have to go through the entire test phases just to eliminate several inert ingredients, and process a *limited number* of medications that could be stamped "Free of Artificial Flavors and Colors" for availability to specific patients, child and adult alike.

The need for strict, unimpaired FDA regulations concerning "new drugs" can't be questioned, but there is no evident reason why the government and the pharmaceutical industry cannot work out an adjustment to rules that will permit *safe* manufacture of small amounts of necessary medicines free of the nonessential additives. Without such adjustments, some manufacturers might find it convenient to duck behind the clauses and avoid production-line changes for what would be a minor portion of total business.

If the food industry can provide approved special dietary products for a minority of individuals who requires them for health purposes, the pharmaceutical industry, far more sophisticated, should be able to meet this specific need without financial calamity.

The problem of vitamins is no less critical, in my opinion, though they are not usually involved in the possible crisis types of illnesses.

A large number of H-LD cases indicate that these patients began vitamins in infancy, the overall infant-care trend for many years. They began with spoon-fed liquid drops, usually artificially colored and flavored, then shifted to the chewable variety at the age of a year or so. Several brands of drops show up like clockwork during the infancy of a number of H-LDs, judging from answers to medical questionnaires.

Whether this incidence occurs because of the popularity of these brands or whether the brands are particularly potent in delivering one or more effects is impossible to determine at this time. It is another area to investigate.

The tasty vitamins of various hues were cultivated by the pharmaceutical industry to replace cod-liver oil, a natural source of vitamins A and B. They do not improve on cod-liver oil, but are certainly more convenient and have a demonstrated sales potency.

Actually, there is great need to question the insertion of the "synthetic cosmetics" into infant vitamins. The color exists primarily for the eye of the parent. If the liquid vitamin has a pleasant taste, the infant will not be very much concerned about the color. In fact, I can't recall any great rebellion against cod-liver oil for infant use during my years in pediatrics.

Facing realism, though, practically all vitamins for children are plied with the "eye and taste bud" additives. Patients, H-LD or otherwise, who react to the synthetics are hard pressed to find vitamin compounds free of the additives. Unless the sales syndrome is deeply involved, industry should be able to flavor infant vitamins with natural ingredients. Most parents would be willing to pay a few extra pennies for natural honey.

Perhaps I am tenaciously conservative in the practice of medicine, but I would not introduce any chemical synthetic, particularly for cosmetic purposes, into a baby's body unless it was absolutely necessary.

# 12

# Letters from Parents

In June 1973 I presented the preliminary findings in dietary management of the H-LD before the allergy section at the annual meeting of the American Medical Association in New York. The presentation caught the attention of a number of medical writers, and considerable national media coverage followed. Within a few weeks, inquiries as well as case histories from parents, doctors, teachers, educators, institutions, universities and government agencies began to arrive at Kaiser-Permanente.

Some of the cases were described in fragmentary paragraphs, others amounted to detailed histories with supporting clinical data from pediatricians or family doctors. As research, the letters were of some value in that they represented a spontaneous cross section of America, one not easily available in the normal course of investigation. They came from every state, from both rural and urban areas, also from foreign lands, at the rate of a hundred to two hundred a week.

To that time, I'd thought I knew something of the H-LD/MBD problem. However, I was not prepared for the sometimes total desperation. "For God's sake, please help," wrote one mother at the end of a five-page single-spaced history of her own eight-year-old Johnny.

Nor was I prepared for the guilt complexes. "What have we done wrong?" Very likely, nothing. Parents cannot blame themselves for the very strong probability of a genetic factor, plus the equally strong probability of environmental factors, of which they have no knowledge and very little control.

The stark human drama-tragedy was outlined in one report, eventually, from the sister of a mother who had surrendered to the H-LD problem in her home. She had attempted suicide with a tranquilizer prescribed for her child.

Their comments, paraphrased here, speak more eloquently than any interpretation I could ever make:

——, who is a very handsome and obviously very bright 4½-year-old child, is the most overtly hyperactive child I have ever seen. I have also never seen a mother who has been quite as distraught and understandably so. The situation, of course, is complicated by the fact that his little sister, a 2-year-old, is being increasingly upset by ——'s behavior. Furthermore, the father is on the road five days a week. When he comes home, he is very controlled and quiet and helpful with —— but by Sunday afternoon he's ready to blow his brains out. The child has responded to medication, but he quickly becomes tolerant to each and every one of them. He has been on as much as 75 mgm of Mellaril a day, up to 40 mgm of Vistaril, Phenobarbital and

Thorazine. His behavior is extremely upsetting just about every place he goes. He just doesn't pick on doctors. For instance, a week ago he went up and down the block where he lives and took the mail out of everyone's box and threw it into the street. At his nursery school, he is now running out into the parking lot where there is a lot of traffic and encouraging other children to 'go with him. He recently, over Christmas, went to visit his grandparents along with other members of the family, and his mother says he left about $1,000 in damages. [Report from a university pediatric neurologist to another physician, called in for consultation]

———

My son, ———, is seven years old. He has an IQ of 130 and is severely learning-disabled. He can't read, write or spell, has severe fine and gross motor involvement, is distractable, hyperactive, aggressive and then some. ——— now attends a small private school for learning-disabled children, but due to his very aggressive behavior we may be forced to remove him. At this point, we have been advised to look into a school for emotionally disturbed children. We are desperate.

———

My seven year old son is currently under the care of a child psychiatrist who had him on Ritalin. Ritalin keeps him controlled for approximately 3½ hours. He takes two a day. He has a high IQ (130) and could do well in school if his attention span was longer. He doesn't get along well with other children because he hits them.

———

My young 11-year-old! Four years ago he went through a clinic in Portland for the MBD children as he was diagnosed and put on Dexedrine much to my objections and this really suppressed eating thus making him much more thin. He has had several complete physical work-ups plus all sorts of IQ tests and as of last week, tested out high school level in IQ. He's giving the school all sorts of fits and they want me to put him back on medication. I'm standing firm this time and refuse to use any more Dexedrine on him.

My eleven year old son has been treated for this for a long time and at present is under no medication. He is very disruptive in school and has a short attention span. Today his elementary school called to say that he is not allowed to have lunch at school but must walk home, rain or shine, because he causes so much disturbance in the cafeteria.

Our son, ———, is six years old and in the first grade of private school. For the past three years he has had excellent private instruction and to date is experiencing no real learning difficulty. His main problem is social in nature. Typically, ——— follows no exact pattern but in reading a list of hyperkinesis symptoms well over 60 percent identify ———'s problem. He has been going to a psychiatrist for two years. He takes 15 mgm of Ritalin in the morning and 15 mgm at noon. It allows him to function more successfully in school and at home. But it does affect his appetite and he's frequently withdrawn. How we would love to get him off it!

Our one child (of six) with the syndrome is a conspicuously large consumer of artificially flavored carbohydrates and soft drinks, is very sensitive (to the point of grogginess) to relatively small doses of Ritalin or Dexedrine. In our experience, such drugs have been of limited usefulness with our youngster. [A psychiatrist]

The more than three thousand communications since midsummer 1973 have drawn various portraits.

Honolulu—I have a hyperactive child. My third one. At times she acts crazy but is extremely bright.

Alton, Ill.—He acts like a wilted flower after taking drugs. [A grandfather]

Houston, Texas—I am totally upset with the treatment my grandson has received. [A doctor]

Johannesburg, South Africa—My seven-year-old son has been seen by several psychiatrists and other specialists, without any noticeable improvement to date. He has been subjected to a large number of tests and has been diagnosed as suffering from hyperkinesis. He is presently being treated with Ritalin, as amphetamines are not available in this country due to strict drug control. He gets what I think are three well-balanced home-cooked meals a day but is a ferocious eater of large quantities of biscuits [cookies], sweets and soft drinks.

Pekin, Ill.—He would like to behave beautifully but says, "It's so hard, Mother."

Very loud, talkative, doesn't reason and must be restrained to dangers (deep water and high places). Sleeps deeper than the other two. Never holds a grudge. Punishment seems nothing to her. Enjoys punishment if not physical.

London—We have an 8-year-old boy (the middle of three children) who seems to have some of the symptoms described, the most distressing being his work at school. His attention span is short. However, there is nothing wrong with his behavior.

Wollaston, Mass.—Ritalin is disastrous for him. Other amphetamines have been moderately successful for him. Please, his life is at stake.

Quebec—We have a five-year-old "holy terror." He can be lovable and adorable sometimes but there are days when I'd like to put him on a slow boat to China.

Pleasant Hills, Calif.—Our eight-year-old is a nervous wreck unless he's on Dexedrine, which he began at the age of five and takes during school terms. We watch him burning himself out like a light.

Australia—He is only 8 years old but we simply cannot control the boy. Ritalin has not worked. Nothing has worked. His hyperactivity is wrecking our entire family.

I've had to hire a reading specialist and now perhaps I need a male person to help him structure his daily activity. [Divorced mother]

---

Fort Langley, British Columbia—We have a ten-year-old boy in level 5 in school, has been on amphetamies for about two years with no noticeable improvement. His scholastic level is more like about grade 2. However, they continually push on him. He is a frustrated, lost boy. We as parents have tried all we can do until we are at wit's end. I am now on tranquilizers and my husband has almost given up.

---

Asheville, North Carolina—I wonder if you really know what it is like to live with ——, never sitting still, into everything, chattering constantly. I love him and I hate him.

---

Norfolk, Va.—He doesn't want to wreck himself. He just can't help it.

If the parents, grandparents and teachers, surfacing at the tip of this international problem, are up against a dilemma, doctors are not far behind. In one photostated letter concerning an H-LD child, a Midwest pediatrician said, believing it, I'm sure: "In most instances, hyperactive behavior in children of a very young age is due to some problem in child-parent relationship." There is no evidence to support this viewpoint.

An Australian doctor advised the parents of the boy who had tried out eleven different drugs: "The child is naughty and you just have to put up with it or sedate the child."

Another neatly washed his hands of it by advising the parents: "Place the child on Ritalin and then put him in a school for the learning-disabled." Poor child!

All of the correspondents who wrote to Kaiser-Permanente were seeking help or information. We prepared a four-page questionnaire, taking in the medical history of the H-LD from the mother's experiences in pregnancy through the neonatal period and up to the present, in hopes of building a large file of case histories which might be helpful in drawing conclusions, and eventually, toward a solution of the entire problem.

We instructed the family doctor or pediatrician to prepare the questionnaire and handle the request for the diet. It would then be up to the doctor to make the final decision for his or her patient. After the initial request, usually by the parent, the program was administered by the doctor involved.

Kaiser-Permanente could not be placed in the position of "prescribing by mail" directly to a patient, nor would I personally prescribe unless I had observed and examined the patient. However, where mail contact was concerned, the foundation offered the service free of charge.

Health plan patients were treated within the normal scope of the Kaiser-Permanente plan. Outside patients were charged the usual consultation rates, but we adopted a policy that no patient would be refused treatment for lack of funds.

Over the next months, reports of success, resulting from the "mail alliance" between far-flung doctors and Kaiser-Permanente, began to land on my desk. Aside from information on the medical questionnaires, and perhaps clinical details in prior correspondence, I knew nothing about these patients. I found myself wishing I could see each child:

Amherst, New York—My daughter is a patient of Dr. ——
who recently wrote to you in regards to your diet. —— is

4 years old and is hyperkinetic. She was taking Benzedrene for six months and I was having good success with it. But then we came across the article in *Newsweek* in regards to this diet. After reading all the information and studying it carefully (which you sent to Dr. ——) I decided to try this diet. I was skeptical but willing to do anything. Within four days I had amazing results. I took her off Benzedrene and really expected all hell to break loose. She was so good I couldn't believe it. I can't remember such a good day with her like that. As each day off medication passed I just couldn't believe this was my daughter. She was relaxed and happy. The only way I can describe it is that she was a real pleasure to have around.

Now she's been on the diet for a month and I am thoroughly pleased with the results so far. I had one set-back and I think I found the cause. I was giving her —— cereal and after a week and a half of eating it almost every morning she became so hyper I couldn't believe it. The only thing this cereal contained was something to prevent it sticking together. My own feelings are there wasn't enough of this ingredient to give off this reaction right away but it gradually built up. The first day I stopped giving her this cereal she was better. I couldn't believe it. Maybe I'm wrong. I don't know for sure but it's the only set-back that I've had.

Something that has really impressed me is that she hasn't had one temper tantrum all the while she's been on the diet.

The reason I am writing this is for some information. First of all, does this diet also mean to omit preservatives? You don't really come out and say so but I've been staying away from them since the cereal.

Also, do you think it is possible to send some menu suggestions? I'm starting to run out of ideas.

What do you recommend in place of aspirin, cough syrup, etc.?

———

Shelton, Iowa—We feel this diet and what it is doing for —— is fabulous.

—— is so interested and so willing to stick to it if *I* have the foods he can eat. If he is in doubt he asks if he can eat it.

On the 5th day of the diet, he said, "Mom, I feel so different." I could hardly hold back the tears because ——'s extreme hyperactivity has caused problems for his sister (two years older) as well as for us.

Very noticeable that he can enter a room and sit down and visit without monopolizing the conversation, antagonizing someone or teasing the dog.

Much more cooperative around home.

His reading teacher told me he has had the best days since he started Jr. Hi.

He does not eat nearly as much as before.

I did not write snacks on menu but when he's with friends, at show, ball games, etc., he eats peanuts and potato chips & buys little cartons of "white" milk.

He burned incense in a new gadget he made in art class and at once reverted to his old behavior pattern. It took us an hour to figure out it was the "perfume." He dumped the rest of the incense out on his own.

In October, after a weekend trip when he had severe problems for 3 days, he said the incense was so thick en route home they could hardly breathe.

After 1 pc. of pumpkin pie Sun. he had problems— couldn't sit or stand—antagonistic, talked constantly, very smart, etc. I asked him if he realized he was upset & he said, "I sure do & it has to be that pie I ate an hr. ago."

I asked him to tell me how he felt & he said, "It's my head."
I said, "Are you dizzy?" & he said, "Sort of. Just feel
strange."

I wrote to —— Foods to see if they could suggest any
other drink. They could only suggest cranberry juice.

It is so apparent that —— feels better when on a diet.
The problem now is for me to prepare meals that are
interesting and also nutritious.

It had to be anticipated that some people would forge
ahead on their own, without physician's advice or recommendation. However, I did not intend to keep the K-P
Diet a secret, nor is there any way to prevent the public
from utilizing *any diet*, with or without medical advice.
I certainly lost no sleep over its usage, since the main purpose is to eliminate synthetics and junk foods.

# 13

# The Story of Food Colors

To place the Johnnys and Jills in their proper space-age frames, and to fully explore the possibilities of chemical "turn-on," it is necessary to go back half a century.

Children of today are certainly no different in normal appetite for candy, cake, cookies, hot dogs and soda pop than the knee-pants brigade of fifty years ago. But along with high-button shoes, Henry Ford's Model T and the biplane, the ingredients of the "goodies" have changed. The difference lies in the modern food supply.

Encompassing practically everything today's child eats and drinks, well beyond the compelling sweet-tooth items, America's food train is well stocked with the nonnutritive intentional additives. They arrive in a bewildering array of categories, and pass in and out of the universal stomach, from cradle to grave.

The history of the massive food-additive industry is a rather typical American story of hard work, ingenuity and occasional recklessness. Beginning in the post–Civil War period, it moved gradually from damp cellar and barn to gleaming laboratories; after World War II it spurted, technologically and synthetically, into the multimillion-dollar business of today.

All allergists, as well as other medical doctors, have wrestled with the subtle additives time and time again in both external and internal disorders. In some way, it has been a losing battle because of the flood of them. One item is delisted by the government; another rises to take its place. One additive doesn't quite do its job of preserving, binding, coloring or flavoring, and the chemists are quick to construct a "better" product.

Prior to the days of Abe Lincoln, there was no formal food industry in the United States. Many people grew what they ate, using natural colorings or flavorings as the only additives—natural juices of fruits and vegetables. Crude time-proven substances and methods were employed for preservation: spices, smoke and salt; cooling or freezing between blocks of sawdust-coated ice. Those who shopped at market stalls could be assured that the products had come out of the ground or off the smoke racks with little alteration.

But with migration to the cities, the pattern of life changed irrevocably and so did the food supply. Enterprise was needed to feed the new city dwellers. Preservatives were required and the old methods were insufficient to handle large quantities of food. Spoiled food meant smaller profits —enter the nonnatural chemical additives!

Food processors dumped everything into food, from formaldehyde, the chemical used to preserve corpses, to borax, which had better use as a cleansing material. Adding to the preservative indiscretions, some merchants took advantage of the consumer's desire for color by merrily tinting pickles with copper sulphate, and candy with red lead that was designed for use on ship bottoms.

There was no government agency to monitor the food supply; no laws to correct the abuses. Suppliers who were caught with their vats slightly acid, mainly by the enraged victim (if he wasn't incapacitated or deceased), usually protested that they were only trying to please the customer, to provide unspoiled, appealing food.

The first solid evidence of food coloring dates to several hundred years before the birth of Christ, with the probability that mineral pigments and vegetable matter were the chief sources. These substances continued to be the primary coloring agents for almost two thousand years. It is a certainty that some human stomachs reacted to some of the mineral pigments, probably the vegetable matter, but little is known of such ailments.

Then, in 1856, Sir William Henry Perkins synthesized the color mauve from coal-tar oil. The coloring industry, as it is known today, began soon afterward. The synthetic dyes quickly proved to be superior, in all commercial ways, to the vegetable and mineral pigments of twenty centuries. Foods dyed with synthetics looked delicious and the public was not often aware that the same dyes they were eating were being used to color the cloth on their bonnets and backs.

By 1900, a total of about eighty dyes made from coal-tar oil were in the American food supply. There are no reliable statistics on the number of deaths or illnesses caused by the indiscriminate use in the period 1870 to 1900, but they likely took a toll, particularly if the hand pouring the color bottle lingered long.

About the same time, Dr. Henry Washington Wiley, chief chemist of the Department of Agriculture, a man who should be remembered with reverence, began crusading. He had the courage to state publicly that "the American people are being steadily poisoned by the dangerous chemicals that are being added to food with reckless abandon."

Finally, in 1906, a Food and Drug Act, the culmination of Wiley's drive, was pushed through Congress and signed by President Theodore Roosevelt. The following year, to the documented moans of many in the industry, enforcement of the new law began, leading to an immediate ban of all but seven of the eighty-odd coal-tar dyes.

A German expert named Hesse had been brought over to sort out the most needed dyes and he selected Orange 1, Erythrosine, Ponceau 3R, Amaranth, Indigotine, Napthol Yellow and Light Green. As time passed, these dyes did not meet all the requirements of the industry, and more were added to the list of those permitted.

In 1973, four basic coal-tar compounds—Triphenylmethane, Azo, Xanthine and Indigo—from which the dyes are made, were still in use. Exhaustive tests have indicated that all four basic chemical structures have either carcinogenic or mutagenic properties. What other properties they may contain remains to be seen or possibly felt.

Of the original seven approved dyes, three still miraculously survive, the others having been delisted as potentially harmful. Amaranth, FD & C (Food, Drug & Cosmetic) Red #2; Erythrosine, FD & C Red #3, and Indigotine, FD & C Blue #2, are hanging in there. (However, Amaranth now appears to be in trouble.)

At last count, thirty-four colors were on the FD & C approved list, in either permanent or provisional status. Of these, ten were coal-tar derivatives. One color, Benzyl Violet, FD & C Violet #1, became a casualty in April 1973. (Of the twenty-four coal-tar colors listed since 1907, fourteen have become casualties.)

Uneasiness and distrust of these chemicals are indicated by the "provisional" listing of most that are approved for human consumption. The rating is precautionary, of course, but it still speaks of long-term uncertainty. Tartrazine first appeared on the government list in 1916, and fifty-seven years later, as FD & C Yellow #5, it could not gain more than a temporary status despite the pleading of the Certified Color Industry.

In one aspect we have not advanced much beyond 1907. In terms of testing, for example, international research has indicated that some of the Azo-family dyes have the ability to produce liver cancer in animals. The Triphenylmethane group has also evidenced cancer-causing properties. Xanthine coal-tar colors are suspected of mutagenic properties.

The length of the period of evaluation and just how these substances act in the human system are the gnawing problem. In parts per million, do they eventually build up and how long does it take? The eating habits of Citizen A could be such that he doesn't really consume a large amount of the parts per million, but Citizen B, on the other hand, might gobble or drink more of the liquid rainbows than his particular system can tolerate. A susceptible individual can get a reaction from a molecular amount.

With these questions largely unanswered, there can be some measure of public gratitude that the lives of the food colors are constantly embattled. The saga of Red 2, Amaranth, is worth telling. Studies in Russia in the late sixties indicated that Red 2 had caused birth defects, fetal deaths and cancer in laboratory animals. This news from Moscow was chilling both to the Food and Drug Administration and to food processors, not to mention cosmetic makers.

At that time, Red 2 was everywhere. It was smeared on lips and floating in medicine. The list of individual items colored by Red 2 was almost endless. As the prime color, or mixed with other dyes, it could be found in candy, hot dogs, jellies, jams, luncheon meats, dry cereals, pickles, pet foods, salad dressings, some soft drinks, processed cheese, cake icings, cough syrup. It was in almost every corner of the supermart, down every aisle, from the "deli" section to home remedies.

FDA tests of Amaranth were begun in the spring of 1971, and by fall, some of the agency's scientists were convinced that hazards did exist. They recommended that the dye be used only for "indirect or incidental applications," such as packaging, and for "external use in drugs and cosmetics."

Five years previously, the Certified Color Industry had petitioned the FDA to remove this same Red 2 from the provisional list and elevate it to the permanent approved list, giving it more than the status of a guest that came to a fifty-eight-year-old dinner.

Industry had a great deal invested in Red 2 and not unexpectedly, it recoiled and volleyed back with its own studies, disputing the findings of the FDA researchers, who had suggested that no more than .075 mgm of Red 2 be permitted per kilogram of body weight per day. That restriction would limit intake to 1.5 mgm per day for a 132-pound human. It would also quickly sweep the supermarket shelves of many profitable items. Coloring could not affect appearance in such a small amount.

Dr. Charles C. Edwards, chief of FDA at the time, referred the volatile question to the Food Protection Committee of the National Academy of Sciences, National Research Council. The committee declined the assignment, but industry pressure forced a reappraisal and the committee, with a previous record of occasionally favoring the additive makers, began the task.

There was little relief at the FDA because some members of the Food Protection Committee were known to have industry ties, and FDA scientists directly involved preferred icy-cold analysis.

The committee report did not surprise most of the working-level FDA scientists. It stated that proposed restrictions were "premature and unnecessary for the moment." The committee concluded that there was "insufficient reason" to reduce the amount of Red 2 in the food supply.

Seemingly, there were valid reasons to question the Russian findings on carcinogenic properties in the dye, and further FDA tests were ordered. The Russians had not carried out certain control factors. But there were not as many reasons to question the Soviet work on "deformed fetuses and fetal deaths." FDA studies found that injection of Red 2 into fertilized eggs resulted in "high death rates, deformities such as incomplete skeletons, defective eyes and stunted growth" in chick embryos.

When this information was presented by an FDA scientist, Julius Coon, Food Protection Committee head, answered, "We all appreciate your coming over here and entertaining us this afternoon."*

Coon had previously remarked: "There is not a shred of evidence or even a basis of reasonable suspicion that any such damaging effects (cancer, genetic effects, birth de-

* Ida Honorof, "A Report to the Consumer," Vol. III, No. 57 (1973).

formities) have ever been caused by the additives or pesticides in food consumed in North America."*

The committee appeared to have based its judgment on the theory that the relationship between animal studies and possible effects on humans is "uncertain," and also on the long-term acceptance of the dye, whose "safe" usage dated back to 1907.

Unless living humans are used as "guinea pigs"—which is understandably frowned on by modern society, and difficult to administer because volunteers are scarce—animal research remains the chief means for testing. To reject animal test findings, conducted by experts under exacting conditions, is to reject the main source of scientific data from which to make evaluations. At the same time, science cannot prove that human and animal systems are identical, in this specific regard. Such argument results in science-industry stalemates.

The government hedged both ways. On July 3, 1972, FDA officials, bucking the advice of the agency's own lower-level scientists, proposed the color be limited to 30 parts per million, which would permit approximately one ounce to each ton of product. The proposal, which was adopted, allowed twenty times the amount recommended by FDA's research. The political clout of the additive industry is indicated by the fact that Red 2 survived, even though restricted.

In the September 1972 issue of *Medical World News*, Dr. Virgil Wodicka, Director of Foods for the FDA, cut to the core of the problem by candidly saying: "We're stuck with Red #2. If we went to the 0.15 milligram limit, we'd wipe out its use."

He continued: "The only unfavorable evidence so far

* *Industrial Medicine*, Vol. 39, No. 10 (October 1970).

advanced is that under some conditions in some laboratories, there is diminution in litter size; all the fetotoxicity tests amount to is that some fetuses are resorbed."

The fetal-death suspicions in test animals and the chick-embryo deformities, as related to Red #2, have never been resolved.

The February 1973 issue of *Consumer Reports*, in its Health & Medicine section, took the sensible approach: "All women of child-bearing age, especially those in the first three months of pregnancy, should consider avoiding artificially colored non-cola soft drinks—unless the label clearly indicates that the product contains no Red 2. That precaution should significantly reduce exposure to the dye without restricting diet or medication recommended by your physician."

Violet #1 did quietly succumb by April 1973. Widely used for some twenty-two years, in beverages and other products, including candy, bakery goods, ice creams, dietary supplements and pet foods, as well as in some drugs and cosmetics, it was "delisted," or banned, as the result of preliminary data from two Japanese studies. Prior research by the FDA and the advisory committee for the National Academy of Sciences had concluded that Violet 1 was safe for human consumption. The Japanese work indicated it might be cancer-causing. Obviously, Violet 1 was not terribly essential to the food supply.

In 1971 the Academy of Sciences estimated that 85 percent of the food colorings used in the United States were made from Red 2; from Tartrazine, Yellow 5, and from Sunset Yellow FCF, Yellow 6, all highly refined from the basic coal-tar compounds.

It is of little comfort to me that these substances are

primarily used for foods which normally require coloring—confections, desserts, soft beverages and candy. *They are the exact "sweet-tooth" delights most popular with small children.*

Sweden properly categorizes the artificial colors and flavors. They are termed "cosmetics" in that country and given the same significance where health is concerned.

A very different investigation into the coal-tar derivatives was carried out in a quiet laboratory of West Virginia University in the Appalachian Mountains, at Morgantown. Under a partial grant from the National Institutes of Health and the National Institute of Allergy and Infectious Diseases, entomologists Tim P. Yoho, Linda Butler and Joseph E. Weaver fed dye additives to adult house flies.

In his paper on the experiment at the Division of Plant Sciences-Entomology, Yoho wrote in 1973: "The wide usage of dye additives in foods, drugs and cosmetics could result in photodynamic injury to man. The potential danger of certain dyes sanctioned by the FDA for use in foods, drugs and/or cosmetics became apparent during a study which utilized the house fly as a test animal."

The phenomenon of photodynamic action had been discovered in 1904 by two German scientists, Jodlbauer and Von Tappeiner. The term describes the usually destructive effects on biological systems when a dye or pigment interacts with normally harmless visible light.

The West Virginians fed flies of both sexes with a milk-sugar diet containing concentrations of the sanctioned dyes, in both dry and liquid forms. Caged, the flies ate in darkness.

When exposed to sunlight, from noon to 3 P.M., or to artificial light from fluorescent tubes, the flies underwent periods of "hyperactivity, characterized by sporadic bursts of flying and prolonged antennal and wing cleaning movements, followed by periods of quiesence." Followed by death!

The project has a bearing on the development of pesticides, but the dyes utilized have nothing to do with pest riddance.

"In flies fed the highest concentration of the most effective dyes, loss of coordination occurred within 5 to 10 minutes, and mortality within 1 hour." No mortality occurred in dye-fed animals in the absence of light.

For comparison purposes, "control" flies, which were fed the milk-sugar diet not containing the dyes, buzzed on and lived out their cycle, in either natural or artificial light.

Fourteen dyes were used in the experiment. Of these, only two, Red 2 and Red 3, are currently authorized for human usage. Violet 1 also participated but is on the banned list. The flies did not react to Red 2 or Violet 1, and the other dyes used are not permitted for direct human consumption, though some are found in cosmetics.

The dye apparently causing the adverse reaction in flies was FD & C Red 3, Erythrosine. It is provisionally sanctioned for human consumption. According to *Food Colors*, a 1971 publication of the Academy of Sciences, Red 3 is used primarily in candies, confections, dessert powders and pharmaceuticals—though in minor amounts, compared to Red 2.

Yoho concluded his paper with: "The fact that photodynamic effects have been observed in many animal systems, including man, indicates the need for more careful scrutiny of dye additives in commercial products."

My thought was impaled on this provocative work at Morgantown for a while, stirred by the descriptions of "hyperactivity," the burst of flying and then submission. It is almost impossible to equate the human system with that of the house fly, yet the possible and interesting implications rose again with a report from Florida in early 1974 that "hyperactivity" appeared to increase in H-LD children who studied or played in intense light.

Of course, the lovely shades of red and yellow and green are not in the food supply simply because of industry salesmanship over a hundred years; they are demanded by the customer. Who wants to eat a sickly-looking bean? Sip muddy cherry? Munch a yellow hot dog?

The colorists have done creditable work. Grandmother could never bake a cherry pie with such a deep, glistening red, mouth-watering before the first bite. Some of the greens in foods are "glossier" than those provided by sun and soil. Mostly, they are 100 percent synthetic.

But one delightful commentary on modern society can be found in canine food. It is generally artificially colored, sometimes to hide other ingredients. The dog, we learn, is color-blind and happily eats what smells and tastes the best. The rich, meaty brown hue in Rover's bowl is for the optical sake of the human owner. Some of the canine and feline medications are colored for the same reason.

Colors in medication are to aid the pharmacist, doctor and patient in identification. Another purpose is eye appeal and psychology, as we have seen. Some patients appear to feel that a medicine is stronger if it is red. Yet, now and then I've found unexpected responses to pill colors.

A young woman of twenty-two, newly married, came to the Kaiser-Permanente allergy clinic with symptoms of asthma. She had had no prior history of the disease that we could discover. The usual allergy tests offered no clues.

Not long thereafter another young woman, also newly-wed, arrived in the clinic with asthma symptoms. We conducted tests with her and could find no reason for the condition, which appeared to date to a few days after her nuptials. Probing further, I asked her to think of all the medications she might be using. She casually mentioned contraceptive pills. I asked about the brand name and obtained a sample. It was synthetically colored.

I contacted the first bride and discovered she was using the same variety. I suggested that both find an uncolored brand, and at last report the brides were living happily-ever-after, having lost their wheezes.

# 14

# The Synthetic Food Flavors

Once upon a time, children had some chance of eating ice cream that contained pure cream, natural fruits and natural flavors, fresh eggs—all scooped into a cone that was composed of natural ingredients. Today's child is likely to lick away at a mound that may involve fifteen synthetic chemicals, mostly used for flavor, and on reducing the mound to cone level, will chew on another chemical-laced article, probably dyed with Tartrazine.

The story of flavoring is more complicated than that of coloring because there are more than a baker's hundred dozen of the artificial flavors. Industry can get by with relatively few colors, but the taste, smell and touch sensations of flavoring require a wide selection.

As with food colors, man began flavoring food with natural ingredients thousands of years ago. But the synthetic-taste industry is again comparatively new, joining the post–World War II technology boom.

There is no known flavor that chemists do not attempt to duplicate and they often come close to matching the true natural flavors. Some companies boast that they can outperform nature. Gourmets can usually detect the difference, but the palate of the general public, now apparently accustomed to the synthetics, seems to make no distinction. Nature, of course, mixes chemicals to arrive at its own flavors, setting some high standards for the lab chemists to follow. The natural flavorings hover around 500 on the United States list.

It is difficult to determine exactly how many synthetic flavors there are in the American food supply; estimates vary from 1,000 to 1,500. Twenty-six were listed in the 1973 Generally Regarded As Safe (GRAS) category, but an additional 714 synthetic flavors were on the so-called Regulated list. The FDA avoids saying they are GRAS. Supposedly, these may be "safely used in foods" in accordance with some rather unrestricted conditions.

By contrast, on last check, France allows exactly seven flavor synthetics, and French food is not the worst in the world.

Confusion is added by the Flavoring Extract Manufacturers' Association (FEMA), stepping into the field of safety judgment. Included on the FEMA list are all the FDA GRASs and Regulated synthetics, plus about 160 additional flavor compounds which do not appear on the government list. The FEMA list has doubtful legal authority.

In flavor enhancing, by category, there are flavor intensifiers, flavor modifiers and flavor potentiators. There are "imitation flavorings" and "artificial flavorings," even "flavor enzymes." Only an expert can keep up with the categories and specific uses. The list of chemicals used in the synthetics occupies almost an inch of a handbook on the additives.

Acetaldehyde becomes black walnut; allyl caproate becomes strawberry; methyl salicylate provides root-beer flavor and wintergreen. As with nature, many flavors are reproduced by a composite of many chemicals, deftly mixed in exacting proportions to create a proximity of the natural chemical. Coffee is said to demand a mixture of more than three hundred compounds.

For instance, though meaningless to most people, yet with a poetic laboratory rhythm of their own, the compounds of artificial pineapple may number seventeen, including allyl caproate, isopentyl acetate, isopentyl isovalerate, ethyl acetate, ethyl butyrate, terpinyl proprionate, ethyl crotonate, caproic acid, butyric acid and acetic acid.

With almost Mephistophelian inventiveness, the chemists can apparently simulate anything from garlic, with allyl disulfide, to sweet peach, with anisic alcohol. In the usage and mixing of the thousand-odd compounds, the food industry appears to face control factors that almost defy current standards and procedures. The heart of the problem is the total amount of compounds in the flavoring relative to the type of product.

Flavor-company executive Richard L. Hall discussed one pertinent aspect in the May 1971 issue of *Food Technology*:

> Both chewing gum and hard candies are of special concern because they are consumed in small amounts which are eaten or chewed gradually over a period of time. Consequently, the level of flavoring per pound of product is very high compared with other food categories . . .
>
> For example, if a flavoring ingredient is used at a level

of 5 ppm (parts per million) in a beverage, an error of 50% in this use level is not serious consequence. But if the use is 5,000 ppm, as it may well be in certain chewing gum or candy products, an error of 50% is significant, especially in terms of the total daily intake of the ingredient in question.

The greatest source of inaccuracy arises from the so-called additive or collective use from several sources. A manufacturer of chewing gum may, for example, add Ajax Cherry Flavor C, Tiptop Cherry Flavor No. 13, and a slug of his own benzaldehyde. He has, of course, no idea of the total benzaldehyde concentration resulting from this combination, since he usually does not know the composition of Tiptop's and Ajax's proprietary formulas.

(On Sunday morning, April 15, 1973, Johnny A awakened early and went out into the garden to help his father. Some twenty minutes later he went back inside and climbed up to the kitchen cabinet, "swiping" two sticks of gum, which he ate on an empty stomach. "Behavior terrible the rest of the day," his mother reported.)

Aside from basic toxicity tests, no one knows very much about the long-term effects, the possible residuals of many of these individual chemicals, let alone the mixing of a half dozen or more. It is believed that most have never undergone more than a "one shot" acute toxicity test and that some have never been tested at all.

Under the 1969 presidential directive to re-evaluate the GRAS list, the FDA is searching literature for adverse reactions. But it is probable that only a small proportion of the synthetics will be submitted to mutagenic, carcinogenic or other acute testing. To rigidly test all the flavoring synthetics currently on the market would take several decades and millions of dollars.

Another problem, insofar as the public is concerned, is that some of the flavors are closely guarded industry secrets, "proprietary formulas," the ingredients of which are revealed to few people. Further, division of responsibility sometimes makes it difficult to determine who is monitoring what product.

Besides Congress, a total of eight different federal agencies and departments are involved in the safety of the food supply: the Food and Drug Administration, the Public Health Service, the Department of Agriculture, the Department of the Interior, the Department of Defense, the Federal Trade Commission and the General Services Administration, and further overlapping is indicated by the Treasury Department's responsibility for additives in alcoholic beverages. FDA sometimes has difficulty in obtaining information when a product is under guardianship of another agency.

Additionally, ropes in the tug of war on the food supply are pulled by industry lobbyists, agricultural groups, consumer groups and health organizations. Where safety is concerned, the FDA has an unenviable job.

However, the swift adverse responses to certain of the synthetics are definitely established and range from the previously mentioned respiratory and skin reactions to gastrointestinal responses. Yet individual reactions cannot be used as a guideline in determining what is good for the population as a whole. Some responses can be obtained from natural chemicals as well as the synthetics. The reactive individuals must persevere and attempt to steer around the chemicals, whether natural or synthetic.

Coping, however, is becoming increasingly difficult for

everyone. A total of 2,764 intentional additives, for direct usage, in packaging or pesticide use in food were listed by the Academy of Sciences, Publication 1274, in 1965. In 1971, industry estimated that the number had grown to more than 3,800.

Hundreds of noncolor, nonflavor additives do odd and often essential jobs in the food supply. In addition to the comparatively few nutrient supplements, there are chemicals to control acidity and alkalinity, foaming, moisture content, firming agents, maturing agents, anticaking agents. There are "buffers" and "binders" and "bleaches" and "texturizers." In the separators, or "sequestrants," there are chelating agents and metal scavengers, emulsifiers and stabilizers. Randomly, sulphur dioxide does its work in dried fruit by helping to maintain color; methyl bromide helps to prevent insect infestation in dry cereals.

The necessity for so many additives is now being questioned. On January 16, 1973, Senator Gaylord Nelson introduced a bill to amend the Federal Food, Drug and Cosmetic Act with the goal of "eliminating the use of unsafe, poorly tested and unnecessary chemicals in the food supply."

Senator Nelson testified: "In 1970, the FDA received 476 new applications for food additives; 62 were approved. In 1971, the FDA received 110 new additive applications; 51 were approved. In 1972, the FDA received 109 new applications, 77 were approved." The birth rate has slowed, but it is still more than 60 a year.

Citing two papers presented at the American Chemical Society's annual meeting in 1971, Senator Nelson projected that "food additive sales will rise from the present $500 million a year to $756 million in 1980."*

What troubles many doctors is the sheer number. When

* *Congressional Record*, January 16, 1973; Vol. 119, No. 8.

a new additive is introduced, it is usually advertised breathlessly within the industry and then presented to the public in slightly different terms. More than one physician then pauses to think: What's really in it?

Promotion is of course a particular American skill, and the additives do not suffer in the exercise of this talent whether for food or cosmetics. They are presented with admirable imagination. For instance, a 1972 annual report to the stockholders of one of the nation's largest flavor and fragrance organizations pictures a human ovum, at the moment of fertilization, on the front cover. Inside, the reader is told: "Flavors and fragrances encourage the use by pregnant women of products which can favorably affect the development and conditioning of the embryo. And during each stage of life thereafter, flavored and fragranced products can aid health and provide pleasure."

I suppose pleasant taste and sweet smell add to the happiness of the mother-to-be, but it is questionable how much effect they would have on the "development and conditioning of the embryo." If they were synthetics, the mother might prefer that they not cross the placental barrier.

At a symposium in late winter 1973, "Drugs and the Unborn Child," sponsored by the National Foundation of the March of Dimes and presented by Cornell University Medical College, Dr. John O. Forfar, of the University of Edinburgh, warned against the indiscriminate use of drugs during pregnancy on the basis of a study involving 911 randomly selected women.

Reviewing the findings, the April 13 issue of *Science* magazine commented: "The symposium highlighted the paucity of our current knowledge of human developmental and fetal pharmacology. Clinicians and researchers are concerned about the possible effects in the fetus—especially about subtle effects, including behavioral changes, that might not be immediately apparent."

The knowledge that "drugs" and the food synthetics are both low-molecular chemicals is also of concern in trips across the placental barrier. Ingestion of them, in large amounts, might have pharmacological and developmental influences on the unborn. Current research would indicate the need for some restraint in imaginative advertising claims.

The bombardment shows even less restraint after the child is born. Slick-paper trade magazines such as *Food Technology* and *Food Product Development* are crammed with lavishly illustrated ads singing the praises and wonders of newly developed additives. Then some of this technology descends with a screech on Saturday morning, the moppet morning on TV, with ZAM-CRACKLE-POP-BANG, some sensationally flavored breakfast cereal, colored an Easter-basket yellow or Frankenstein green.

Chances are that the cereal will be loaded with synthetics. Or the commercials might be promoting a new candy bar or new fruit-flavored or chocolate-flavored drink. Most likely, there will be little or no pure fruit or natural chocolate in either one.

As target for a number of reputable food and drink manufacturers, and their ad-agency account executives, the children later show up on sales charts. I have an idea they are also beginning to show up on charts of an entirely different nature.

On my kitchen bulletin board is a newspaper cartoon from the *Wall Street Journal* depicting a food executive talking to his plant manager. The caption reads: "We'll have to call that latest shipment back. What with the preservatives, artificial flavors, sweeteners, artificial coloring and all, we left the food content out."*

Rather predictably, somehow sadly, Saturday morning's Los Angeles *Times*, January 19, 1974, front-paged an interesting double headline: "SOME CANDY BARS HAVE MYSTERY COATING" and "WHATEVER IT IS, IT'S NOT CHOCOLATE." The article then stated:

> Chocolate bars and Almond Joys have a lot in common. Chocolate is not one of them.
>
> Peter Paul, Inc., is now coating Mounds, Almond Joy, and other confections with an undisclosed brown substance touted by the company as having a "better shelf life" than chocolate.
>
> Consumers finding that distasteful can chew on this: for years, the coatings on the Curtiss Candy Co.'s Baby Ruth, Oh Henry! and Butterfinger bars have been made with oil derived from a plant—the cotton plant.
>
> "It's a more lasting coating," said Gerald Doolin, of the National Confectionery Association. "Nice gloss, nice shine, nice snap to the product." Not to mention, as Peter Paul President Lloyd W. Elston points out, "better shelf life."
>
> Elston denies that the compound coating his candy comes from cotton but will not say what it is. "It's contents we haven't divulged," he said, adding, "I'm not exactly sure what it is."
>
> Elston says he is confident the brown stuff "handles, looks and tastes like a chocolate product."
>
> "The difference is a rather technical one," he says.

Nice gloss. Nice shine. Nice snap.
But what is in it?

* S. Hattis, Wall Street Journal: 1973.

# 15

# How Safe Are
# "Safe Additives"?

The additives go along quietly enough, stirring and whirring in the factories and then circulating through the food supply until one is challenged to a sudden halt; then the whole family of synthetics appears to shiver for a few months. Once composure is recovered, industry usually fights back by maintaining that the "animal tests" were not reliable or that the whole thing was politically inspired.

Cyclamates, the noncaloric sweeteners, were considered "safe" until 1969. Within the group of cyclohexylsulfamates were calcium cyclamate, magnesium cyclamate, potassium cyclamate and sodium cyclamate. They were used to artificially sweeten such items as canned peaches, soft drinks, apricots, pears, cherries, fruit cocktail, figs and pineapple, fruit preserves and jams. They were also combined with saccharin.

Then the FDA revealed that tests had shown gross abnormalities in chick embryos developed from eggs injected with the sweetener. It was the end of the cyclamates for the time being, but the resilience of the industry is indicated by continuing efforts to resurrect them. They were profitable. That ledger heritage seems to outweigh the fact that they were also proven potentially dangerous.

On October 30, 1969, Arthur T. Schramm, one of the leading spokesmen for the additive industry, addressed a letter to the National Academy of Sciences: "The entire atmosphere growing out of TV programming, news reports about scientific experiments conducted with cyclamates and MSG (monosodium glutamate), coupled with politically oriented Congressional Hearings and careless statements by apparently qualified publicity-seeking individuals, is one of economic terrorism. I have been asked by the Food Protection Committee to secure time for qualified members of the scientific community to put this matter in proper perspective for the public."*

In 1957, Mr. Schramm had said of food colors: "Man in his present generation has inherited a wealth of mechanical conveniences to supplement his quest for fuller satisfaction of his higher nature. Whether he realizes it or not, these conveniences are not without cost—that cost being the element of risk. The most impressive example of man's willingness to expose himself to hazards for a convenience is his continued use of the automobile. Were the automobile considered in the same manner as certified colors, the shocking toll of 42,000 killed in 1956 would most certainly demand its delisting."

Man has only one body to last a lifetime. One stomach. One nervous system. He can discard ten bodies from Detroit. Food is a necessity, not a matter of choice or con-

* Ida Honorof, "A Report to the Consumer," Vol. III, No. 46.

venience, and cannot be equated with an automobile in terms of risk.

Additionally, the time-honored idea that synthetic additives can be judged simply from routine carcinogenic and mutagenic standards is out of date and dangerous. Advances in medical science would indicate that neurological and behavioral effects must now be added to the examinations. It is folly to assume that a synthetic chemical, declared free, within limits, of acute toxic properties, is also automatically free of damage to various body systems.

In safeguarding the food supply, there is constant and understandable hedging in a number of areas. The unanswerable question of "how safe is safe" is involved, and tests are only positive to a point. Certainly, the government could not go beyond its Generally Regarded As Safe classifications of 1958 and 1960, updating a 1938 bill.

But a listing, and then a label classification of "government approved" or "U.S. Certified," usually imply to the buyer that he or she is purchasing an article which is guaranteed safe by the government. *No such guarantee is made.* Nor can it be made. The key is: *generally regarded* as safe.

In man's natural desire to quickly satisfy "taste and mouth feel," as well as "eye appeal," he has constructed his own additive environment. Industry has capably responded, urged on by a booming population, by the necessity to process foods at the lowest possible cost, and by tomorrow's even greater demand for convenience foods.

An estimated eight thousand different edible items can be found on the giant-sized supermarket shelves and in meat cases during a given week; drugs are also numerous. So the task of determining and monitoring the safety of food and drugs, in all forms, is monstrous, almost unmanageable. It is also subject to great economic stresses. The latter factor poses the largest threat to health in the race to create new products, or to modify old ones; to have them tested quickly, and beat the competitor to the counter.

Now, our entire food economy—production, processing, promotion and sales—is locked into the intentional use of additives. Without them, the food supply would no doubt stop within a few weeks. The whole multibillion-dollar industry, from growing fields to the table, would probably collapse. *The additives are here to stay*. It is now a question of safeguard and management.

Looking both at the present and the future, Senator Abraham Ribicoff, opening hearings in April 1971 on "Chemicals and the Future of Man," said: "With these foods we each consume every year more than four pounds of chemical preservatives, stabilizers, colorings, flavorings and other additives. And the amount of these artificial substances is increasing each year. Their use has doubled in the past fifteen years from 400 million pounds to 800 million pounds.

"These developments raise three basic questions: (1) How much do we know about the hazards to human health from these chemicals? (2) How much assurance of chemical safety should be required? (3) What must the Federal government do to assure that the chemicals we absorb are safe?"

Medical science must answer the senator's first question: Relatively little.

The answer to the next question should be: Enough chemical safety to be reasonably certain that the average human can ingest them over a lifetime without undue risk to health.

The answer to the government-regulation question should

be: More comprehensive toxicity tests; additional tests and prolonged observations for behavioral and other systemic effects to remove as many risks as possible to health, welfare and the pursuit of happiness.

The Ribicoff statistics were updated and revised by Senator Gaylord Nelson in his January 1973 introduction of the bill to amend the Federal Food, Drug and Cosmetic Act: ". . . more than one billion pounds today, according to industry figures. The industry says that the average American eats 5 pounds of additives every year."*

Usage had grown by two million pounds in twenty-one months, if the Senate figures were accurate.


In the past twenty-five years, the march away from the home kitchen has increased from a trickle to a tide, and moving with the human wall are the convenience foods—bound together by the synthetic additives. Without them, the freezers would be bare; vending machines empty. We are back to the "locked-in" environment.

Additionally, a federal labor forecast predicts that over 130 million American females, the traditional overseers of the family kitchen and diet, will be employed full time by A.D. 2000. Undoubtedly the chemical food industry will stand ready to meet the demands for quick foods in as short order as possible and with products of unbelievably complex nature. Hopefully, by that time, man will know more about the biochemistry of the additives.

Industry has already indicated its ability to help meet the world's inadequate supply of food proteins by such steps as development of synthetic chicken, synthetic bacon and

* *Congressional Record*, January 16, 1973; Vol. 119, No. 8.

synthetic beef from soybean proteins. But one of the most disturbing aspects of the trend is the almost religious zeal of some of the synthetic-food advocates. They are ecstatic with the prospects.

Others take it in stride. In his book, *The Chemicals We Eat*, Melvin A. Bernarde matter-of-factly discusses foods of the future and suggests that protein from petroleum might be on the supermarket shelves in the 1980s. "Oil companies have long known that microbes can grow on a diet of crude oil. Bacteria and fungi are often found on the bottom of oil storage tanks, in oil-impregnated soils, and even under tar-surfaced roads . . . As the population grows and land becomes scarcer, raising meat animals is a more and more expensive way of producing protein. For example, a 1000-pound steer can produce about 1 pound of usable protein a day, while 1000 pounds of bacteria can produce 4000 pounds of usable protein in the same length of time.*

Meanwhile, the oil companies are experimenting. Packaged "Exxon" beef? The technology is probably available for production, but I doubt that it is available for proper testing.

A million or more years have gone into the development of the superb and intricate machinery of the human body. From my point of view, it is a little too much to ask these mechanisms to accept such radical environmental changes in a period of a little over a hundred years. Penalties have already been exacted and will continue to be exacted.

One somewhat ridiculous public relations argument of the additive industry is that the whole human body is chemical; that all components of food are chemical; that we live in a total natural chemistry, even without synthetics; that

* New York: American Heritage Press, 1971.

the synthetics themselves are simply amalgamations of our total chemical environment.

The simplest answer is that water is a marvelous chemical but doesn't mix well with another marvelous chemical known as oil.

Another claim, and far from ridiculous, is that we are consuming these additives in such infinitesimal amounts that they cannot possibly harm us. Our systems can take them in stride, handle and excrete them. How could anyone be affected by something of 300 parts to the million? Unfortunately this hypothesis, this grand guess and brave gamble, cannot be disproved in many cases. Time alone will answer it unless batteries of tests are forced by the federal government, almost certainly against the will and political clout of the additive makers.

There is, however, a general argument to the thesis that these tiny amounts are of no appreciable significance in the human body. When asked what amount of a compound is required for sensitization in the human system, Nobel Laureate Linus Pauling, the eminent Stanford University scientist, replied succinctly, "A single molecule."

Molecules vary in size, but a million small ones can be gathered on a pinhead. As another example, three or four might be contained in a nanogram, one billionth of a gram.

*We cannot safely predict that any part per million or billion or trillion will not have an effect on certain individuals or on all individuals.*

Until we obtain more facts, we really don't know what is going on in the human brain or in the nervous system, and how chemicals, both natural and synthetic, might affect these mechanisms. Therefore, there can be no snap answers from medicine; no soothing assurances from the chemical food industry or the FDA.

The human body, whether it houses an H-LD/MBD or a nonreactive individual, is deserving of the utmost possible care. It should not join plastic cups and pop-top cans on the list of technology's disposables.

# 16

# Genetics and Behavior

Quite obviously, if the exact cause of H-LD/MBD were known, the problem would not exist or at least would be under some semblance of control. Thus far, it has stubbornly defied medical science, staying beyond reach despite dedicated efforts, particularly within the last ten years. Remaining unsolved, it provokes the usual marked differences of expert opinion.

Dr. Arthur Benton, University of Iowa neurologist, believes that a hypothesis of "major cerebral abnormality" should be adopted. Dr. Michael Gazzaniga, New York University psychologist, theorizes that "MBD may reflect problems of shuttling information between specialized processing centers of the brain." Both of these qualified investigators may be wholly or partially right or completely wrong.

There are many other beliefs. There is a concept that the problem is based on incomplete maturation of the brain at birth and in early infancy. It is generally recognized that the degree of development of the brain varies from infant to infant. On this basis, some observers argue that H-LD/ MBD is actually delayed brain maturation, preying on some children, skipping others.

There is the oft-used, oft-quoted school of thought that connects the various forms and degrees of complications during pregnancy—toxemia, medications, injury, resulting in physical insult to the fetus brain; and complications during delivery—prolonged labor or other delivery problems, such as premature placental separation, which can result in injury to the infant brain.

Other observers draw on the impaired intelligence and behavioral disturbances associated with certain hereditary conditions: phenylketonuria (PKU); Turner's syndrome— retarded growth and sexual development, low posterior hairline margin, increased carrying angle of the arms; X-chromosome involvement; Klinefelter's syndrome—abnormality of sex chromosomes with the presence of small testes.

Genetic predisposition, combined with biochemical aberrations, surfaces repeatedly in surveying the studies on causes. There is always rather strong suggestive support that H-LD/MBD might well be genetic.

For myself, I linger on the statement by Dr. Bert N. LaDu that each "person has his own biological individuality that determines a pharmacological individuality." Simply, it means that each person possesses a unique body structure which will determine how she or he will react to many types of chemicals—in drugs and foods, even those that pollute the air.

To fully appreciate this mechanism, the hereditary features that individuals have in common, as well as the variations, must be considered. We are all a bit more complicated

than the "shinbone being connected to the leg bone" and
the heart pumping around the clock. The human body is a
remarkable, skin-draped, biochemical machine.

The basic functional elements of all body tissues are the
proteins, made up of mixtures of basic elements which include primarily carbon, oxygen, hydrogen and nitrogen.
Additionally, trace elements such as iron, copper, sodium,
sulphur, magnesium and phosphorus are also incorporated
into some protein structures.

These basic elements occur in various proportions and
in different arrangements to form the twenty amino acids
that are the building blocks of all proteins. They are uniform
throughout nature, joined end to end to form groups called
peptides. So proteins are actually chains of peptides consisting of a variable number of amino acids, ranging from
a hundred to three hundred or more. Each protein has its
own characteristic sequence of amino acids.

In discussing a protein and its behavior in body chemistry,
many questions must be answered. How large is the molecule
in question, and how many peptide chains and how many
amino acids are there? In what order are the amino acids
arranged?—*a very critical factor in genetics*. Does the protein molecule consist of only one large peptide chain, or
are two or more peptide chains linked together? What is
the shape of the molecule and how flexible is it?

Fundamentally, all animals, including man, have a basic
protein structure, which is coded and determined by the
genetic structure, the composition of the genes. Those proteins, or groups of proteins, contain all the coded information required for development, growth and functioning of
the individual. In some manner yet unexplained, all the
necessary data for this performance are programmed into
the substance of the genetic protein, indicating that nature

had a pretty good computer under way before man ever lived in caves.

In turn, the genes are linked together to form a chainlike structure called the chromosomes. These reside in the cell nucleus. The chromosomes are constant for each species of animal. In man, there are normally forty-six chromosomes, consisting of twenty-two pairs plus two sex chromosomes, occurring as XX in females and XY in males. The genes of each chromosome have specific functions, but so far as the human species is concerned, the greater majority of these functions remain a mystery.

The basic genetic pattern, the fundamental structure of the individual in each individual species, is handed down from generation to generation according to its specific genetic code. This pattern determines how the individual will develop. It chooses the sex, the texture and color of skin and hair, and the entire body configuration, as well as the manner in which the body will function.

This inherited genetic structure, the body design and engine model, also determines how the individual will react to any influence, whether internally or environmentally, i.e., externally. On the basis of this concept, the performance of any organism is the expression of interaction between the functions programmed by the genes and all environmental factors.

At a casual glance it would appear that all individuals inherit identical genetic patterns transmitted by their progenitors, the kindly or unkindly, healthy or unhealthy ancestors of the species. However, on closer examination it is revealed that there are constantly occurring variations in the structure of the gene protein. The variations are better known, of course, as mutations. Very often the mutation may be the substitution of only a single amino acid out of several hundred within the protein structure of the gene.

Mutations occur frequently, but not all are passed on to future generations. Many mutations disappear on the death of the individual who owns them, in the inexorable dust-to-dust cycle. However, mutations that *are* passed on to future generations through heredity become the genetic variations of the individual.

For better or worse, richer or poorer, the offspring, that bawling new baby, does not inherit 100 percent of the characteristics of both parents. It is impossible. There is a random mixture of genes passed along, provident for the human race. The father may predominate or the mother may override. However, most of the time the child inherits a fairly equal number of traits from both parents. Due to the random mixture, though, the child does not inherit every variation from the parents. It is usually a hit-and-miss situation.

Further, a variation that is handed down may remain completely silent, producing no reactions, until it encounters a specific chemical which triggers a disturbance. Many previously mentioned adverse reactions to drugs or food synthetics have exactly this genetic basis.

It is my firm belief, a theory based on observation of the more than one hundred children that I have personally treated with the K-P Diet, plus others who have responded under guidance of their own pediatricians, that this is the circumstance which exists with a genetically predisposed group of the H-LDs: *Children within this specific group suffer adverse reactions triggered by one or more chemicals contained in the synthetic flavorings and colorings.*

I can find no other reason for the "turn-on" and "turn-off"

conditions induced by controlling the ingestion of the chemicals. Of course, it follows that *children who do not inherit the variation do not react to the chemicals*.

Additionally, since food additives are identical in basic structure to drugs—both low-molecular substances—there is reason to believe that the triggering reactions are somewhat the same.

Several well-known and specific examples of the behavior of drugs serving as triggers can be found in the field of pharmacogenetics, a specialty about ten years old dealing with the variations in the actions of drugs governed by genetics.

One action involves a disease known as Zurich hemoglobinopathy and I must touch briefly on the technical aspects despite its awesome terminology. The ailment, partly named after the city in which it was first described, is a form of anemia affecting the hemoglobin (the iron-and-oxygen-carrying fractions of the red blood cell). Hemoglobin is structured of four chains: two A-chains consisting of 282 amino acids, and two B-chains of 292 amino acids. The four chains are twisted together to form the hemoglobin molecule.

In the Zurich sickness, there is a single genetic variation at the sixty-third position of the amino acids in the B-chains of hemoglobin. Simply, there has been a mix-up perpetrated by nature. At that sixty-third position, genetics has substituted arginine for the normally occurring histidine. Both are basic, essential amino acids.

This alteration goes along silently, unknown to the individual, causing no problems whatsoever, until a drug like Sulfanilamide, an oxidant, enters into the system. Then the mechanism malfunctions and severe anemia is the result. Another person in the same family may not have this variation, this amino-acid substitution, and will not be bothered by the drug. Genetics can play damnable tricks!

There is another drug-induced anemia dependent upon a variation occurring in the X, or sex-linked, chromosome. Primiquine, an antimalarial drug, can set off a disturbance in individuals unfortunate enough to inherit this variation. It involves an enzyme of glucose metabolism known scientifically as glucose-6-dehydrogenase. Since the X-linked chromosome is concerned, *males* usually develop an adverse reaction to Primiquine. This is another example of the trickiness of genetics.

Male selection in this disturbance strongly suggests that the preponderance of male H-LDs may also be genetically sex-linked. A number of disorders that occur almost exclusively in males have already been explained on the basis of the X-chromosome involvement.

In fact, I think that many of the characteristics of the H-LD/MBD can be explained by genetics. The more frequent occurrence of H-LD among children with normal or high IQs has a distinct genetic possibility. The same explanation can be applied to the involvement of only one child in the family, the usual circumstance.

Pointing a finger at genetic variations as the possible root of the problem means an extremely wide distribution of these alterations, wide enough to cover the estimated 5 million children in America. It also raises two possibilities: 1) that the variations are indeed widely distributed, and 2) that it is polygenic, involving many chemicals.

The possibility of this width is clearly demonstrated by experiences with another drug, Isoniazid (INH), used for the treatment of tuberculosis. Very early in the use of the drug, clinicians observed a high frequency of adverse reactions. This was soon explained on a genetic basis.

It was learned that almost 50 percent of the patients, due to an inherited pattern, could metabolize, or break down, the drug very quickly. The remaining 50 percent were slow in metabolizing it, resulting in an accumulation which in turn brought on adverse reactions. Otherwise, aside from their variations, and their commonly shared TB, they were normal individuals. The significance of the finding was that *one-half* the population, a tremendous percentage, had one genetic pattern; the other half, another pattern. Both halves were normal, but they were different.

Still another profound example of genetics keying disturbances is the infrequent Lesch-Nyhan syndrome. It is described in medical literature with pointed reference to "behavior." At the time of the discovery, in 1964, Dr. Michael Lesch was a student resident at Johns Hopkins University, and Dr. William L. Nyhan was on the faculty. The patient involved was a four-year-old boy. They were able to determine that the cause of his abnormal behavior was an inherited molecular disease associated with defective uric-acid metabolism.

The uric-acid disturbance of the disease is not at all relevant to the H-LD, but the behavior patterns of the syndrome are sometimes similar in nature. The patients are extremely aggressive on occasion and delight in hitting people. During some periods they have to be placed in arm splints to prevent horrible self-mutilation. They welcome the restraints. They don't want to bite themselves, as they do.

On other occasions they are rather well behaved and seem to understand their "turned-on" condition, caused by overproduction of uric acid. Dr. Nyhan said, "They are bright. They apologize quickly when they know they have done something wrong. They laugh when something funny occurs." Hospital personnel understand them and become quite fond of them.

Of the unbridled compulsive aggression Dr. Nyhan said, "One is tempted to think of this disturbance as fingernail biting with the volume turned up."

The Lesch-Nyhan syndrome cannot be applied specifically to the H-LD, yet it stands as the first behavioral disorder explained on the basis of a biochemical aberration linked to a genetic alteration.

It challenges medical science to answer the question: How many other forms of compulsive behavior, even outright aggression, have genetic and biochemical foundations?

# 17

# The Need for Research

Naturally, the anguished parents of the H-LD child often feel that nothing is being done to solve their problem, that science is too busy in other undertakings, from space shots to heart disease and cancer research. Doctors don't understand! Education doesn't understand! Teachers are not sympathetic!

I've sensed the mixture of frustration and anger in many conversations. Yet there is considerable work going on in many fields, much of it not readily visible.

Many facets are being researched. The National Institute of Mental Health has already supported several projects in the areas of behavior and prenatal toxicology. With the theme "Behavioral Toxicity," the Fifth Rochester International Conference on Environmental Toxicology explored the methods of evaluation of behavioral toxicity in both man and laboratory animals.

Among the environmental pollutants discussed were carbon monoxide, dieldrin (a pesticide), lead and methyl mercury. At first glance, none of these would appear to have any direct bearing on the H-LD. Yet in 1972, a team from the Department of Psychiatry and Pediatrics, State of New York; the Downstate Medical Center, Brooklyn; and Southbeach Psychiatric Center, New York, reported higher levels of lead in blood of urine from hyperactive children as contrasted with nonhyperactive children.

It was concluded that there is an "association between hyperactivity and raised lead levels; that a large body-lead burden may exert consequences that have been hitherto unrealized; that a definition of what is a toxic level for blood-lead needs re-evaluation; that physicians should look for raised lead levels in children with hyperactivity."

Much the same concern was voiced by Dr. Jane Lin-Fu in the December 1973 issue of the *New England Journal of Medicine* in a definitive study on lead exposure. "There is mounting evidence that many children who have undue lead absorption but never overt lead poisoning later give evidence of minimal brain damage such as hyperactivity, perceptual handicap and impaired fine motor incoordination."

Dr. Lin-Fu named environmental sources, from infancy on, such as canned milk, paint, dust, newsprint and auto exhaust, pointing out that exposure levels not thought to be dangerous were in fact capable of subtle, yet irreversible damage.

Important? Any medical finding has possible importance and should be followed until dead end or success. The lead findings may be extremely important to one group of H-LDs or all groups. The evidence again points to the possibility of an infinitesimal amount of environmental hazard having the capability of a "turn on."

. . .

The FDA is also under way with research toward development of animal models for determining the psychotoxicity potential of food chemicals. Other laboratories have similar studies in progress.

Supplementing all of this rather specialized research is the ongoing work in psychology and psychiatry, in diagnostics, in drug management and alternatives to drug management. There is vast research in progress on a multiplicity of levels in education to improve the learning-disability remedial programs as well as special teacher training programs. There is also the final "on-scene," nitty-gritty level in the special remedial schools, centers and clinics, with the H-LD/MBD only a chair and desk away.

As a whole, between federal, state and private agencies, and through grants to dozens of institutions in numerous related fields, there is an unprecedented effort being channeled toward aiding this stricken child. Dismaying, though, to all concerned, is the realistic time factor involved in the entire research effort. Even with high priorities, the designing of "cause and effect" studies and controls, the development of the models and finally the testing phases could take years.

For instance, narrowing the area to food additives as a possible cause for some patients or attempting to establish a cause-effect relationship on a compound-by-compound basis might take from ten to fifty years simply because of the number of chemicals involved (more than two thousand estimated for possible direct ingestion). The cost would also be considerable.

Meanwhile, any delay, whether two years or ten, will see the graph move steadily upward if current statistics are at all valid. Another million hyperactive–learning-disabled children could be struggling for survival at the end of five years.

It was precisely for this reason—the lack of signs of any early solution—that I recommended the empirical application of dietary management to the H-LD, following what I considered to be sufficient substantiating evidence that the synthetic additives were involved.

Obviously, any hypothesis that deals with a medical or social problem should be thoroughly tested if the testing can be accomplished at a reasonable cost and within a reasonable amount of time. This hypothesis meets both prerequisites.

For instance, eleven children, ranging from three years to seventeen years in age, who were enrolled in a family-care center in Redwood Valley, California, were placed on the K-P Diet on May 13, 1974. They all had problems. Eight were wards of the court, removed from their natural parents. Five of them had been institutionalized in a state hospital with diagnoses varying from autism and emotionally disturbed to neurologically handicapped. Each of the eleven children had behavior or learning difficulties.

After two weeks of strict food control under twenty-four-hour supervision, six of the children had responded favorably to dietary management; two showed suggestive responses. There was no improvement in three cases, of which two had been diagnosed as autistic. The only variable from their past routine was the elimination diet. The twenty-four-hour control factor was of prime importance in this test.

In late spring 1974 a short-term demonstration program in the Santa Cruz, California, school system was sponsored and funded by the Department of Education under State Superintendent Wilson Riles. Twenty-five children were included in the study, a number of whom were on medication. The study involved a psychologist, a nutritionist, a teacher coordinator, the teachers directly concerned with the children, plus parents who cooperated in varying degrees. The particular school was in a disadvantaged area.

An evaluation of classroom behavior and scholastic achievement will be made by the school psychologist, following completion of the study, for comparison against the previous month; home behavior for the same period is to be evaluated by the parents. This short-term study will serve as a prototype for adoption by other schools in other areas.

Analysis of classroom behavior and scholastic achievement is being made for comparison against the previous month. Home behavior is also being studied from parent evaluation. The short-term Santa Cruz study will serve as a prototype for adoption by other schools. The cost is relatively minor, administration simple.

Of the twenty-five children participating in the study, four responded dramatically, twelve displayed a favorable response, while nine did not respond. However, the majority of this latter group failed to adhere strictly to the diet, defeating any worthwhile evaluation of the failures.

Another study was derived from children reporting to the Pediatrics Department of the Santa Clara Kaiser-Permanente Medical Center. Following pediatric evaluations, nurse practitioners guided the parents and supervised the K-P Diet. Ten children indicated a very favorable response to diet management; four were able to discontinue drug therapy.

Sponsored by the National Institute of Education, a broader-based academic study is being designed at the Human Resource Institute of Boston, under direction of Dr. C. Keith Conners, associate professor of psychology in the Department of Psychiatry at Harvard Medical School. This program will be a double-blind cross-over control study under supervision and evaluation of a trained team of psychologists, psychiatrists, educators, allergists and nutritionists. Each child will have a psychological and scholastic evaluation before, during and after completion of the period of observation.

The Boston program, for which I will serve as consultant, will permit the gathering of more definitive conclusions regarding the behavior for each child—at home, at school and from interaction with peers.

So many intriguing questions hang over the H-LD/MBD. What is the current rate of incidence in the Little Red Schoolhouse, if such a welcome institution still exists? What is the rural rate versus the urban rate? What is the H-LD rate in schools in extremely remote areas—say, Tikigaq school in the Eskimo whaling village of Point Hope, Alaska? What is the rate in England? In Russia? In China? In Japan?

Russian statistics would be of particular interest. There are very few synthetic additives in the Soviet food supply. Soft drinks, of the popular American type, are just beginning to become available in the major cities. Chewing gum is only now reaching the gates of the Kremlin.

Studies are needed to identify the genetic pattern that is liable to predispose the H-LDs. What is this pattern that makes them susceptible to one or more environmental hazards? Once the pattern is known, observations in the fields of biochemistry and immunochemistry can be patched in. It is unlikely that any single field can provide the answers.

Further, I fully believe that as man begins to understand the full implications of genetic variations, he will begin to understand the susceptibility of every human to certain environmental factors. Medical science can then guard against them.

Although it smacks slightly of George Orwell's *1984*, I hope that sometime in the future *every child, at birth*, will have a computerized genetic pattern from which to predict, throughout a lifetime, exactly what environmental factors are likely to influence his or her well-being and behavior. It may be man's only future protection against rampaging technology. Orwellian aspects aside, such a computerized pattern could contribute materially to the welfare and happiness of the human race.

Precise long-term pedigree mapping in humans would be extremely difficult and take years. The cost would be in the millions. As a stop-gap measure, a mapping of the immediate family might be helpful. As an example of this, we are contemplating a genetic study utilizing a sample of identical twins, gathered from throughout the state of California, to determine whether or not both twins manifest hyperkinesis. In nonidentical twins, it is conceivable that one reacts to the hyperkinesis of the other.

I think there is also a great need to take a clinical look backward at the H-LD whenever possible. In certain areas, that is already being done. Any information developed has a potential of value.

Over a period of thirteen years, Kaiser-Permanente has collected data on 21,000 pregnant women. Out of those, 19,000 live births were recorded. Unfortunately there are no data on diet during pregnancy, but there is information on drugs. These data must be correlated to determine if there is an application to H-LD children within the mass of 19,000 births. A huge job? Yes, but perhaps worth the effort.

Thirty-thousand children are computerized for various data in the Kaiser-Permanente Multiphasic Program. A percentage, not yet determined, are hyperkinetic. The data on them must be extracted for comparison purposes. Massive task? Yes, but worth an attempt.

Much smaller research, at my request, is being planned with a group of eighty mothers who had received quantities of artificial flavors and colors in a controlled diet during pregnancy. The flavors and colors were not administered by design but rather appeared in the normal course of this study, done for another purpose.

There are many similar pools of potential data existing in medicine, not designed for research on the H-LD/MBD but now of possible value. I believe they should be studied in the quest of all possible avenues.

Oddly enough, I feel optimistic. If the general public becomes completely aware of the width and depth, the searing tragedy, of the H-LD/MBD, momentum and public money will be added to the existing attack, and the solutions should be within reach. Whatever amount of money is spent will be saved many times over. Of more importance, the waste of millions of children whose learning is disabled will stop or at least be brought under control.

I am even optimistic in my own special field of interest concerning the H-LD versus food additives. Dynapol, a company in Palo Alto, California, is working on polymers as a substitute for coal-tar colors. If developed, they will pass through the body without breaking down and entering the system. They will be excreted in the same form in which they were ingested. Some gums already have that capacity.

If Dynapol can achieve a polymerized chemical which can serve as a dye, it will be a major breakthrough, and possibly of profound benefit to all mankind.

# 18

## The Pollutants We Ingest

I would guess that the nagging thought—a question, really —began forming shortly after I dietarily treated the Oakland "hives" patient and received the totally unexpected response of nonaggression. Over the years, in quiet moments, I toyed with the question, examining it, occasionally speculating when going through scientific literature of various disciplines, arrested by some finding on a related subject. Then it narrowed and took shape while I observed the H-LD children, trying to gain some understanding of possible cause and effect.

I finally formulated it for myself: *Aside from the worn, tried-and-true factors—mechanization, pell-mell pace of modern living, and overcrowding, socioeconomic conditions —are there other widespread environmental factors that might also be at the root of man's steadily growing tendencies toward unprovoked aggression and violence?*

In hopes of finding an interpretation of the H-LD observations and applying it in a broader sense, my own field of immunology offered a direction in which to search.

The unraveling of the defense system of the body—immunity—did not take place until the early fifties when immunologists, principally Dr. Robert A. Good, studied the behavior of the body's protective mechanisms in lower animals. Observations in the primitive forms, particularly of that sacrificial barnyard inhabitant, the ordinary chicken, permitted the separation of some of the intertwined complex systems that occur in higher animal forms, very much including man.

Guided by this work, I studied the recent findings in the field of comparative ethology, the science of animal behavior. The importance of this branch of science to health was finally recognized with the award of the 1973 Nobel prize in medicine to Emil von Frisch, Nikolass Tinbergen and Konrad Lorenz.

In the introduction to his brilliant book *On Aggression*,* Lorenz states: "Aggression is an instinct like any other and in natural conditions it helps just as much as any other to insure survival of the individual and the species. In man, whose own efforts have caused an *overrapid* change in the conditions of his life, aggressive impulse often has destructive results."

Overrapid, of course, links to both territorial overcrowding of the human species, and the grating, grinding pace of living in a technological society. It also describes, with thudding understatement, what has occurred in a few short years, relatively, in the advance from the hand-cranked adding machine to the computer; the stereopticon to television; the Pony Express to Telstar; the Wright brothers to lunar

* New York: Harcourt, Brace & World, 1963.

landings; Browning machine guns to hydrogen bombs, in what might be the finale of another type of violence.

Inevitably, Lorenz's concept of "overrapid" change applies to the intentional introduction of synthetics into what man eats and drinks; the chemical by-products in the air he breathes; the synthetic pollution of the soil in which his food is grown; the chemical wastes in his lakes, rivers and oceans. In terms of life, man changed his environment overnight.

Through the processes of evolution and selection over a period of a million years or more, *Homo sapiens* made his first appearance about forty or fifty thousand years ago. From his emergence up to about 9000 B.C., primitive man lived in a completely natural environment, wandering about in the search for natural food supply.

Finally, with the development of agriculture and animal husbandry, he began to settle down and display his inventiveness. Developing new varieties of grain, improving on the wild grains and domesticating the animals, he largely gave up the nomadic existence.

Psychiatrist Erich Fromm points up the monumental significance of this conversion in his recent book, *The Anatomy of Human Destructiveness*.* Dr. Fromm contends: "It would not be exaggerated to say that the discovery of agriculture was the prelude to all scientific thinking and later technological development."

But the early development was slow and gentle in terms of both stomach and thinking processes. Changes came gradually over several thousand years. It permitted adaptation to the environment and enabled the human system to accept changes in diet and the new mode of living. With the improved food supply, man was able to develop tribes, cities

* New York: Holt, Rinehart & Winston, 1973.

and nations. These, too, developed slowly. Compared to the twentieth century, the pattern of environmental change was like sand blowing on rock. Man was again permitted to adapt genetically to the alternatives he had created in nature.

At times, as centuries crawled by, an individual would appear whose genetic pattern would not fit into the new environment. This individual perished, leaving only a breed of man who could tolerate the altered environment. This breed, becoming present man, also had the good fortune to move along at turtle pace and adjust accordingly.

Then, by about the middle of the nineteenth century, environmental changes had picked up dazzling speed in comparison to all other centuries. In the 1760s the steam engine had been invented by James Watt, and Sir Richard Arkwright had perfected the use of steam power for his spinning Jenny, replacing slowly working human hands in the weaving industry. Soon the industrial revolution was worldwide.

With industrial development, great changes occurred rapidly in the distribution of the population. Agriculture no longer dominated. Overcrowding of the cities, now the source of labor for factories, resulted in inadequate shelter and inadequate food supply, leading to socioeconomic problems never before faced by man. The conditions, in turn, began to influence behavior in an entirely different way.

If the total speed of the nineteenth century was dazzling, the last quarter of the 1800s gathered even new momentum, flashed past 1900, and then reached higher speed following World War I, going to a relative human "mach" after World War II. Looking back nine thousand dim years, it is almost incredible that the human frame and intellect has survived the past one hundred and twenty-five years.

In the evolution of man, a hundred-plus years of technology torrent are as insignificant as a polyp on a coral reef. But applied to living in the last half of the twentieth century, they are cataclysmic to behavior. Man has not had adequate time to adapt to the changes and new environment, physically or mentally.

All of the changes, mechanical and chemical, have twisted the physical environment as well as the social environment out of all recognition from that of only a few hundred years ago. With this in mind, Tinbergen said: "As a result, our behavioral organization is no longer faced with the environment in which the organization was molded, and as a consequence, misfires."

The disruptive consequences of "misfiring" now threaten the very existence of the species: pollution and depletion of natural resources, population explosion, social stress, constant shadow of nuclear war.

For centuries, all his socioeconomic ills have seemed to influence the behavior of man. Yet these factors do not now provide the complete answer to the sharp upward curve of aggression and violence in the past twenty-five years. The ghetto can no longer claim sole ownership. The attack by fist, knife and gun has spread to the stamping grounds of the middle class and into wealthy surburbia; the snarl of frustration and rage spills out universally and from unlikely mouths.

Without question, socioeconomic pressures influence instinctive behavior, and such behavior becomes imprinted on the patterns of the individual. It is rather easily identifiable and does not need a psychologist's explanation. Deprived infanthood and adolescence can add up to troubled adult. But explanation is definitely needed when aggression and violence begin to detonate far away from the misery of the ghetto.

. . .

To date, mechanization—the noisy, smoke-generating turning of wheels and gears—has been blamed for the social stresses and for specifically influencing man's behavior. But another leading aspect of technology—chemical production—has largely gone unnoticed. Brother to the machine, silent chemistry escaped attention until man began to examine the atmosphere and look at his rivers. That has happened within the past twenty years.

Chemistry, of course, did not stand mute and idle after the mid-eighteenth-century industrial revolution began. Pacing other fields, sometimes far ahead of them, this science industry has now provided millions of compounds which have never before appeared in nature.

In 1971, the Stanford Research Institute, under contract to the National Cancer Institute, began work on a system to rank chemicals by their estimated hazard to man. I have been informed by Mr. Arthur McGee, who is in charge of the SRI studies, that since 1839, when organic chemistry began, approximately 3 million chemicals have been synthesized—compounds which never existed in nature. Of these chemicals, it is estimated that over 30,000 are currently in use for all purposes (industrial, medicinal, agricultural, etc.). Although 5,000 of these compounds have had some tests for carcinogenicity, only 2,000 have been "reliably tested" as to whether they are a cause of cancer.

Of the 30,000 chemicals in use today, over 3,800 occur in our foods as additives. Some of the additives have been studied for carcinogenesis, mutagenesis and blastogenesis, but not a single one of the synthetics used in our food has been subjected to the rigid investigations required for licensing drugs.

Phasing them in and out as needed, man has created this

mass of substances in less than a hundred and fifty years. How much he really knows about the chemicals, for either industrial or food use, cannot be readily answered—very little in all probability. However, the Stanford research is the first attempt to systematically rank them for hazard.

It may be regrettable that we have waited until the 1970s to ask the mass of chemicals: Are you harmful to touch and breathe, eat and drink?

The immediate benefits of all the synthetics to mankind is incalculable, but along with the benefits, as usual, is a certain cost, to paraphrase the additive-industry lobbyist on the subject of automobiles and food colors. In view of the speed with which the synthetics overtook man, bestowing comfort and pleasure and profits beyond comprehension, it is understandable that he did not stop to calculate the price. He woke up one morning, in the 1960s, to the realization that he had been presented the bill by Mother Nature. He had polluted his atmosphere, his food and water supply, in a little over a hundred years. He may now be awakening to the possibility that within the same synthetics, particularly those he ingests, could be some answers to the behavior "misfirings."

In this rude dawn and uneasy period of questioning, it is not too surprising to find that the rapidly developed food synthetics have been introduced into the fuel that operates the human body with little public awareness. Realization often comes only at the precise moment of reading the fine print on a food-package label.

The time is now long overdue to look at these chemicals, not only in regard to the H-LDs but in regard to the human species as a whole. It is time to coldly question whether or not some of them have the possibility of disrupting the normal neurological pathways.

So little is known of the nervous system that even conjecture about the mechanism is difficult. However, it is known that a number of natural chemicals in the body operate on the nervous system. They include serotonin, dopamine, norepinephrine and epinephrine, a class of substances derived from amino acids and called biogenic amines. They are found throughout the body, particularly in nerve and brain tissues. They are considered to be neurotransmitters, meaning that they carry impulses at nerve junctions—from one nerve to another. The same quartet of biogenic amines exist in lower animals. Man is not that far removed from four-legged creatures.

It appears that there is a definite relationship between aggression and the amount of serotonin in the brain stem. If a normal rat is given a drug which stimulates the production of serotonin, the rat becomes aggressive; if the serotonin is decreased, the aggression is modified. The drug is apparently a control factor.

Serotonin, a nerve-impulse transmitter, offers a wealthy field for research in behavior alone. Recently Drs. John J. Fernstrom and Richard J. Wurtman, of the Massachusetts Institute of Technology, reported that "when a meal rich in carbohydrates is eaten, the brain manufactures more serotonin." They estimate that the brain reacts within twenty to thirty minutes.

They further state that "the mechanism may be part of a closed circle in which diet influences food consumption." Another finding was that "the ratio of carbohydrates, protein and fat in the diet had a definite relationship to the amount of serotonin in the brain."

It is galling to know that these substances occur in the brain and other nerve tissues and yet not know how they interrelate and function. Perhaps the reason their functions remain a mystery is that they are only a part of an intricate system of "mediators," many of which have not been identified.

The problem of identification is ably illustrated by the studies of Dr. Roger Guilleman, of the Salk Institute for Biological Studies in San Diego. Attempting to determine what amount of thyrotropin releasing factor (TRF), the hormone that stimulates the thyroid, is required to create activity in that gland, Dr. Guilleman and his associates began work on 5 million fragments of sheep brains weighing more than 500 tons, and containing, eventually, 50 tons of hypothalmic fragments, the hypothalmus being situated at the base of the brain, in man and animal alike.

From this mass of 50 tons Dr. Guilleman extracted one milligram of pure TRF and then found that this product was active and stimulating at *1 to 5 nanograms*, 1 to 5 billionths of a gram. In the pituitary culture systems, he found that the product was active at *50 picograms*, or 50 trillionths of a gram.

I remain stunned by the exquisitely infinitesimal amount of activator—stunned that any substance of 50 trillionths of a gram could react in the human body.

But the work flatly indicates the problems and intricacies encountered in attempting to study the various mediators in the brain and the nervous system. "There are other mediators to be identified," said Dr. Guilleman.

To do so will require considerable scientific ingenuity and many man-hours of research. Until more parts of the puzzle are known, the riddle of the nervous system and behavior of man cannot be fully explained.

However, it is generally accepted that each animal has a number of instincts. Each instinct is dependent upon the activity of a nervous center which controls a great complex of responses. The instincts do not operate independently but are involved in an overwhelmingly complex system of mechanisms which regulate animal life in its many forms. They protect the individual against adverse influences from the environment and enable maintenance as a living organism.

The nerve complex is the same in the lower animal as it is in man. The chief difference in the two is that man has a highly developed brain center, which gives him a unique intellectual superiority over all creatures of the animal kingdom. The brain actually serves as a highly developed and complex computer which is initially programmed by genetics, and then modified by environmental influences—*learning*.

In addition to the brain, there are also scattered about the body a number of automatic centers and control areas which send out a constant flow of impulses to the various organs as well as to the central nervous motor mechanisms. The summation of these actions constitutes *behavior*.

The flow of impulses from the automatic centers is constant, but there is an *innate releasing mechanism* (IRM) which acts as a control. It is conceivable, even probable, that the IRM prevents an excess of discharge into muscular active cells. Otherwise there would be complete chaos in the body—supercharging, the motor running wild.

As the third and final step of my hypothesis about the H-LD, it is this intricate regulating system that is being disturbed by some of the food additives, the familiar low-molecular chemicals, particularly the artificial colors and flavors. To the point of redundancy—they are in the "drug" family, cousins to the same drug used to excite serotonin in the rat's brain.

To restate the entire theory:

1. The hyperactive disturbance is nonimmunologic. There is no natural body defense against it.

2. Those children who react to the synthetic additives have genetic variations—not abnormalities—which predispose them to such adverse responses. It is not the child's fault, nor are the parents responsible for this quirk of nature.

3. The innate releasing mechanism is involved in the disturbance.

While the aggressive patterns are manifested in a group of H-LDs apparently genetically prone to the reactions, I also have reason to believe that the pattern is not confined to the H-LD.

The food supply is a common environmental factor, jointly utilized by the aggressive teen-ager and aggressive adult, as well as the H-LD. The two former groups, if genetically inclined, have no more defense against the chemical "turn ons" than do the unfortunate H-LDs.

In attempting to understand man's increasingly aggressive behavior, no environmental factor, especially synthetics brought on by technological spurts, can be excused on face value.

Contrary to the courts of law, none can be declared innocent without full trial.

In addition to the thousands of synthetic chemicals in our food supply, the search over the past two decades for unidentified dietary factors has taken on a new and unexpected direction. On closer view we are becoming aware that the awesome chemical landscape of carbon, oxygen, hydrogen and nitrogen, which make up the proteins, fats and carbohydrates of the body, is dotted with many trace elements. These trace elements at times occur in concentrations of parts per billion (ppb) which are several trillion atoms per gram and a comparatively large number of atoms for each body cell.

Prior to 1957 seven essential trace elements were known: iron, copper, iodine, manganese, zinc, cobalt and molybdenum. To these have been added another seven: selenium, chromium, tin, vanadium, fluorine, silica and nickel. The recognition of these trace elements has contributed to the emergence of bioinorganic chemistry as a separate category of research which is opening new possibilities in biochemistry and medicine.

Some of the natural trace elements may make contributions to the behavior of man, either by presence or absence, deficiency or overabundance. Until we have some true understanding of their roles, we have little chance of knowing what their interactions might be with the ever-widening family of synthetic chemicals.

The new discipline of orthomolecular psychiatry, a term coined by Dr. Linus Pauling, is psychiatry predicated upon the interaction of chemicals and the homeostasis, or balance, of chemicals within the body. All of the human psychological processes are dependent upon the proper balance, the concentration of various chemicals inside the cells and outside of them. If an imbalance occurs, malfunction may develop.

It is quite possible that orthomolecular psychiatry will at last force a re-evaluation of "emotional disturbances" and perhaps help put an end to diagnostic arguments between emotional and organic factors. Insanity is a disease of the brain, not a matter of intellect. No one knows why the imbalance takes place, nor how it works, but medical science is slowly groping toward the answer.

With this groping, it would appear vitally necessary to carefully examine both the natural and synthetic chemicals in our food supply and attempt to learn how they interrelate, with a view toward providing as much total health safety as possible.

Man easily discarded the Model T and biplane as technology no longer of use. It is now similarly wise, within the food-man equation, to discard the idea that toxicity is the only standard upon which to make judgment of food safety; to strongly question the idea that aggression is largely the result of nonorganic factors.

With a steadily growing population, planning for the future food supply—which depends more and more upon the vast group of synthetics—must take into account the total well-being of man, which most certainly includes his behavior.

As the energy crisis has luckily, even kindly, brought the waning years of the twentieth century face to face with the harsh facts of natural-resource extravagance, perhaps the suffering of the embattled Jills and Johnnys—incomparable natural resources—will have served a good and lasting purpose by forcing science to explore all facets of their problem.

# THE K-P DIET

Two groups of foods are eliminated by the diet:

Group I is made up of a number of fruits and two vegetables (tomato and cucumber). This group of foods contains natural salicylates (see page 7).

Group II is made up of all foods that contain a synthetic (artificial) color or flavor.

Consult the general instructions on page 175 before beginning the diet.

There are no tests to determine whether a child will show an unfavorable behavioral response to any food item in either Group I or II. The allergy skin tests for foods are not applicable to this problem.

In the absence of tests it is necessary to start the diet by eliminating *every* food that might disturb the child, from Group I and from those foods not permitted in Group II.

## GROUP I

This is the list of fruits and vegetables that contain natural salicylates. They must be omitted in any and all forms—fresh, frozen, canned, dried, as juice or as an ingredient of prepared foods.

| FRUITS | VEGETABLES |
|---|---|
| Almonds | Tomatoes and all tomato |
| Apples | products |
| Apricots | Cucumbers (pickles) |

FRUITS

Berries
   Blackberries
   Boysenberries
   Gooseberries
   Raspberries
   Strawberries
Cherries
Currants
Grapes and raisins or any
   product made of grapes,
   e.g., wine, wine vinegar,
   jellies, etc.
Nectarines
Oranges (*Note:* grapefruit,
   lemon and lime are per-
   mitted)
Peaches
Plums and prunes

If the child shows a favorable response to the K-P Diet, after four to six weeks the foods in Group I may be slowly restored. The intolerance to these foods is usually related to aspirin-sensitivity. Since aspirin sensitivity in the child is difficult to detect, a history of such intolerance in the parents is used as a guide. If one or the other parent offers a history of aspirin-sensitivity, caution must be exercised in reintroducing the fruits and vegetables in Group I.

Try the foods *one at a time* for about three or four days. If no unfavorable reaction in the child's behavior is noted, another food item can be added. This procedure is followed until all items in Group I are tested and those to which there is no adverse reaction are restored to the diet.

## GROUP II

All foods that contain artificial color and artificial flavor are prohibited. The following list is meant to serve as a guide for shopping and food preparation.

It should be emphasized that this diet is not concerned with food preservatives except for Butylated Hydroxy Toluene (BHT). An occasional child may show an adverse response to BHT.

All foods that contain artificial color and artificial flavors are not listed. Such a list is not practical. Do not use *any* foods that contain these substances.

*The safest approach is to carefully read the labels.* Upon checking in the market, a number of items will be found to contain *no* artificial color or flavor.

There are some permitted food items that must be prepared at home to avoid synthetics.

*From present indications, an individual sensitive to artificial colors and flavors must avoid them throughout his life.*

| NOT PERMITTED | PERMITTED |
|---|---|
| CEREALS | CEREALS |
| All cereals with artificial colors and flavors<br>All instant-breakfast preparations | Any cereal without artificial colors or flavors, dry or cooked |
| BAKERY GOODS | BAKERY GOODS |
| All manufactured cakes, cookies, pastries, sweet rolls, doughnuts, etc.<br>Pie crusts | Any product without artificial color or flavor, but most bakery items must be prepared at home |

| NOT PERMITTED | PERMITTED |
|---|---|
| Frozen baked goods<br>Many packaged baking<br>   mixes | All commercial breads ex-<br>cept egg bread and whole<br>wheat (usually dyed)<br>All flours |
| **LUNCHEON MEATS**<br><br>Bologna<br>Salami<br>Frankfurters<br>Sausages*<br>Meat loaf<br>Ham, bacon, pork* | **ALL MEATS** |
| **POULTRY**<br><br>All barbecued types<br>All turkeys with prepared<br>   basting, called "self-bast-<br>   ing"; prepared stuffing | **ALL POULTRY EXCEPT<br>STUFFED** |
| **FISH**<br><br>Frozen fish filets that are<br>   dyed or flavored; fish<br>   sticks that are dyed or<br>   flavored | **ALL FRESH FISH** |
| **DESSERTS**<br><br>Manufactured ice creams,<br>   unless the label specifies<br>   no synthetic coloring or | **DESSERTS**<br><br>Homemade ice cream with-<br>   out artificial coloring or<br>   flavoring |

* When colored or flavored, usually indicated on the package.

| NOT PERMITTED | PERMITTED |
|---|---|
| flavoring; the same applies to sherbet, ices, gelatins, junkets, puddings | Gelatins—homemade from pure gelatins, with any permitted natural fruit or fruit juices |
| All powdered puddings | |
| All dessert mixes | Tapioca |
| Flavored yogurt | Homemade custards and puddings |
| | Plain yogurt |

| CANDIES | CANDIES |
|---|---|
| All manufactured types, hard or soft | Homemade candies, without almonds |

| BEVERAGES | BEVERAGES |
|---|---|
| Cider | Grapefruit juice |
| Wine | Pineapple juice |
| Beer | Pear nectar |
| Diet drinks | Guava nectar |
| Soft drinks | Homemade lemonade or limeade from fresh lemons or limes |
| All instant-breakfast drinks | |
| All quick-mix powdered drinks | |
| Tea, hot or cold | Seven-Up |
| Prepared chocolate milk | Milk |

| MISCELLANEOUS ITEMS | MISCELLANEOUS ITEMS |
|---|---|
| Oleomargarine | All cooking oils and fats |
| Colored butter | Sweet butter, not colored or flavored |
| Mustard | Mustard prepared at home from pure powder and distilled vinegar |

THE K-P DIET

| NOT PERMITTED | PERMITTED |
|---|---|
| All mint-flavored items | Jams or jellies made from permitted fruits, not artificially colored or flavored |
| Soy sauce, if flavored or colored | Honey |
| Cider vinegar | Homemade mayonnaise |
| Wine vinegar | Distilled white vinegar |
| Commercial chocolate syrup | Homemade chocolate syrup for all purposes |
| Barbecue-flavored potato chips | |
| Cloves | |
| Catsup | |
| Chili sauce | |
| Colored cheeses | All natural (white) cheeses |

SUNDRY ITEMS

*Practically all pediatric medications and vitamins contain artificial color and flavors.* When medications are required, a physician should be consulted.

Most over-the-counter medications contain aspirin, as well as artificial flavors and colors, e.g., Aspirin, Bufferin, Excedrin, Alka-Seltzer, Empirin, Empirin Compound, Anacin.

All toothpastes and toothpowder*
All mouthwashes
All cough drops
All throat lozenges
Antacid tablets
Perfumes

* A salt-and-soda mixture can be used for cleaning teeth. Neutrogena soap (unscented) can be substituted for toothpaste or powder.

## General Instructions

1. Keep a diet diary. Note down *everything* the child eats. It is recommended that a diet diary be kept even after the child shows a good response.

In the event an unfavorable characteristic of the behavioral pattern recurs, the diet record will serve as a checklist to determine whether an infraction has occurred.

Infractions should be rare when the diet is carefully monitored. When they occur, the symptoms may reappear within two to four hours.

*Whenever a change in behavior occurs, suspect an infraction.*

Along with the diet diary, it is usually helpful to record the behavioral and scholastic responses.

2. Any fruit or vegetable not on the prohibited list of Group I is permitted. Occasionally a child may have an individual intolerance to a food item. When suspected, the food should be eliminated. For example, a child may not tolerate a cereal with the preservative BHT (check the label), or some types of potato chips.

3. All package and container labels should be carefully checked. For some foods the term "flavor" is used without specifying artificial or natural. In such cases, *do not* use the item. If in doubt, do not experiment.

4. Most "permitted" items are available in the markets. It is usually not necessary to pay premium prices at specialty food stores.

5. There are no restrictions placed upon reasonable quantities of sweets, which are important to most children. To avoid artificial flavors and colors, it is usually necessary to prepare such items at home. These include most baked goods, e.g., cakes, cookies, pies, pastries and puddings.

Practically all candies on the market have artificial colors and flavors added. Candies can easily be prepared at home (see suggested recipes).

Ice cream must usually be prepared at home. There are some natural ice creams on the market, but their availability varies with different regions. It is advisable to check carefully with the manufacturer. Inquire specifically about colors and flavors. Do not be satisfied with the term "pure."

6. The greatest success is observed when the entire family adheres to the diet. This should present no special hardship, since the diet is quite varied and liberal. It should be noted that the initial restrictions concern only some fruits and two vegetables. In the majority of cases these fruits and vegetables can be restored to the diet after about four to six weeks. The elimination of the nonessential additives is frequently beneficial to the other members of the family— both children and adults.

When the prohibited foods are not around the house, temptation and the risk of infractions are eliminated. The all-out effort by all family members serves as an added incentive for the child.

7. The diet must be adhered to 100 percent. Compliance of 80 percent or 90 percent can lead to failure. It is important to remember that often a single bite or a single drink can cause an undesired response which may persist for seventy-two hours or more. An infraction on Sunday and then again on Wednesday can keep the child in a persistent state of disturbed behavior throughout the week.

8. On the average a good response will be observed within seven to twenty-one days. In some children the favorable response will be noted as early as the first week, but sometimes as late as seven weeks.

9. When behavior-modifying drugs have been prescribed, *a physician should always be consulted before making any change in the medication*. In most cases the drugs can be discontinued within two or three weeks, even with a history of administration of the medication for many years. However, this judgment must be determined by the physician.

10. After the diet has been started, the behavior-modifying drugs will occasionally stimulate instead of quiet the child. If so, consult a physician.

## Food Preparation

I am not a cook, nor a gourmet, nor at all handy in the kitchen. But I enjoy good, wholesome food, and I was fortunate enough to marry a lady whose many talents include superiority in the kitchen. Often, Helene Feingold imaginatively reaches gourmet heights, but she is also a thrifty chef. In the early months of the diet program Helene heard me talk about the problems of food preparation without use of synthetics. She began to collect recipes and experiment with her own originals. The recipes that follow were gathered from relatives, friends, and friends of friends. She tested each one in our kitchen, and I served as my own test animal in this research, a very willing "guinea pig" for whatever came off the stove. I thrived throughout the whole experience. What follows is Helene's creditable work, not mine.

To assist in implementing the elimination diet, sample menus and recipes have been compiled with the idea of aiding the sometimes harried mother in the kitchen as well as at the grocery counter. Some of the recipes are old, some new, but all are family favorites and usually old-fashioned, since they are all cooked at home. None are complicated or difficult and are submitted to demonstrate that the diet permits great variety.

In addition to menu suggestions, extra recipes are included to offer ideas for experimentation. The menus for large family meals are intended to serve only as a guide and can be revised to suit your needs.

Pasta and noodles are sometimes dyed, particularly the egg variety. The ingredients of these products are usually not listed on the package. In most large urban areas there are local manufacturers of pasta products. If a local product is used, its ingredients can easily be checked with the manufacturer.

To make shopping easier, it is suggested that a list be prepared of generally used products that contain no artificial flavors or colors. It can serve as a handy reference. However, it is a good idea to check the ingredients periodically even on the items you buy routinely. Manufacturers often change the ingredients in the "additive game."

## TIME, MONEY AND STEP SAVERS

The menus to follow are planned so that several items in the meal can be cooked at one time, to save energy for the housewife and the oven. For example, when boiling rice for dinner, cook enough so that you have ¾ cup left over for rice pudding at a later meal. Plain rice with sugar and cinnamon or milk or cream is a simple but good dessert.

If possible, shop once a week for staples and fill in with perishables when they are on sale. That way, you can really concentrate on watching labels carefully.

If the family does not eat the crusty end pieces of bread,

keep them in a freezer to use as bread dressing or bread pudding. They can also be fried in shortening to make croutons to be served with pea soup or added to green salads.

Small pieces of leftover chicken or pork, when combined with a few bean sprouts and bits of green onion, make a perfect addition to eggs for Egg Foo Yong. Make sure to serve with natural soy sauce.

Candies made at home serve several purposes. The child enjoys helping and "licking the spoon and pan" as well as enjoying the final product. Icing on cakes will also help to satisfy sweet-tooth needs. Bread and butter with sugar or honey is a perfect sweet snack.

Cinnamon toast is another old-fashioned, grandmother's treat. Have a jar of sugar already mixed with a little cinnamon to be used on toast instead of jelly.

A bar of Baker's German Sweet Chocolate is a marvelous substitute for a so-called candy bar that is loaded with synthetics.

Making ice cream from the many available recipes can be another old-fashioned family-participation treat with the H-LD supervising the cranking.

Keep popcorn in the freezer or refrigerator. It pops better when cold. Good for snacks.

Plan menus so that there is something tempting left over for the next day's school lunch.

Saturday is a good "Bake Day," when children can participate. Choose another day or late afternoon for candy making. One of the lost joys is sampling, and children, on any diet, need to find fun in food.

There are many excellent hams on the market, without a color additive, and they make a great dinner as well as provide sandwiches for school lunch. Tongue can be used instead of ham, on occasion.

There are several good pork-sausage products available without coloring or flavoring. Labels must be carefully examined.

Gelatin salads may be made from Knox Gelatin. Use permitted fruit juices.

There are some pie shells on the market minus flavoring and coloring. Lemon, banana or custard filling can be used, as well as chocolate, pineapple or pumpkin. All of these, of course, must be home prepared.

For a super H-LD birthday party, serve chicken legs instead of hot dogs. Buy the legs with the second joint attached. It is less expensive, easily available, and the second joints can be saved for the next day. The legs can be marinated in soy sauce (unflavored variety) and sautéed.

For the H-LD girl, bake an angel food or other white cake. Decorate with white icing. Place a small glass in the center of the cake in the hole made by the tube; fill it with a small bouquet of garden flowers. Petals can be placed on the cake itself. Colorful and different for any party!

For a boy's H-LD birthday, use lemon, pure caramel or "home" chocolate icing; decorate the sides with small paper animals for each slice. Avoid plastic animals.

Holiday dinners can be planned with all the favorite foods, without the chemical synthetics. It will take a bit more time and care, forcing return to "fresh" cranberries, for instance. But not a single food of the traditional variety has to be missing from the table. An exception would be hot dogs for the Fourth of July, but hamburgers with a homemade relish will do the trick.

Save beet juice for coloring Easter eggs (the usual manufactured dyes are "turn-ons"). To decorate the Easter ham or lamb, hard-boil a number of eggs, peel them and let cool, then place them in a glass jar with beet juice from canned beets. Keep in refrigerator overnight. They are most attractive and safe to eat. Good for lunches and salads at any time.

# Sample Menus
## to Be Used as a Guide
(ITEM MARKED WITH AN * DENOTES RECIPE OR
COMMENT BELOW)

### MONDAY

| BREAKFAST | SCHOOL LUNCH | DINNER |
|---|---|---|
| Grapefruit juice | Chicken or | Chinese meatballs* |
| Mixed dry ce- | chicken salad | or plain ham- |
| real,* with milk | sandwich | burgers |
| Chocolate milk | made with | Chinese style vege- |
| made with | homemade | tables* |
| homemade | mayonnaise* | Baked bananas* |
| syrup* | Relishes— | |
| | olives, car- | |
| | rots, celery or | |
| | radishes | |
| | Cake, milk | |

### AFTERNOON SNACK

Party mix* and chocolate milk

**BREAKFAST**

Mix your own dry cereals and serve with brown sugar. Use
equal parts of Quick Cooking Quaker Oats, Grapenuts,
Shredded Wheat, broken into tiny pieces. Any three or four
cereals can be used if they contain no artificial color or
flavoring. If the child is doing well after four weeks, sliced
nuts may be added. Watch the reactions carefully.

182

CHOCOLATE SYRUP

| | |
|---|---|
| 2 cups sugar | 2 tablespoons cornstarch |
| 1 quart water | Pinch of salt |
| 4 ounces Baker's unsweet-ened chocolate (4 squares) | 2 teaspoons pure vanilla |

Boil sugar and water until it is syrupy, about five minutes. Add chocolate, and cornstarch dissolved with a little water, and a pinch of salt. Stir until chocolate is melted and syrup is smooth, another five minutes. Add vanilla when cool, and store in a glass jar for use all week. Syrup must be refrigerated to keep fresh. Use 2 tablespoons of syrup for each glass of chocolate milk or hot chocolate. May be used for sauces or as toppings on custard or desserts.

LUNCH

Use homemade mayonnaise on all sandwiches.

MAYONNAISE

| | |
|---|---|
| 1 teaspoon salt | 1 tablespoon distilled white vinegar |
| ½ teaspoon mustard pow-der | 1 egg, unbeaten |
| 1 teaspoon sugar | 1 cup salad oil |
| 1 tablespoon fresh lemon juice | |

Put dry ingredients into mixing bowl, add lemon juice and vinegar. Add egg but do not beat.

Add ⅓ of the oil and beat with wheel beater until mixture begins to thicken. Add another ⅓ cup of oil. Beat for 1 minute. Add rest of oil and beat for another minute.

There are many other home prepared mayonnaise recipes, some for blenders, that are very quick.

**DINNER**

CHINESE MEATBALLS

| | |
|---|---|
| 1 8¾ oz. can crushed pine-apple | 1 egg |
| 1 lb. ground beef or lamb | ¼ cup milk |
| ½ lb. ground pork or veal | ¾ cup oatmeal |
| 1 small can water chestnuts | cooking oil |
| 3½ teaspoons soy sauce (read label) | boiling water or stock |
| 1½ teaspoons salt | ⅓ cup brown sugar |
| ¼ teaspoon ginger | 3 tablespoons white distilled vinegar |
| | 2 tablespoons cornstarch |

Drain pineapple, reserving liquid. Mix thoroughly the pineapple, meats, diced water chestnuts (very fine), 1½ teaspoons of the soy sauce, 1 teaspoon of the salt, the ginger, egg, milk and oatmeal. Shape into medium-sized balls. Pour enough oil to cover bottom of a large skillet. Add meatballs and brown on all sides.

In a bowl, add enough boiling water to pineapple juice to make 1½ cups (if available, use pure chicken or beef stock. Do not use cubes that contain synthetics). Add sugar, the remaining soy sauce and salt, and the white vinegar. Pour the liquid over the browned meatballs in the skillet and simmer for 25 minutes. Remove meatballs from skillet and add the cornstarch mixed with a little water to the liquid in the skillet. Cook over low heat while stirring, until thickened. Return meatballs to the sauce and reheat. Serves 4 to 6.

CHINESE STYLE VEGETABLES

| | |
|---|---|
| ½ lb. fresh bean sprouts (or canned, well drained) | ½ lb. fresh mushrooms |
| 2 large onions | Peanut oil for frying |
| 2 zucchini (or any other vegetables available) | Soy sauce free of color or flavor |

Put 2 tablespoons Planter's Oil or any desired peanut oil in a large heavy frying pan and heat.

Cut vegetables into bite-size pieces; do not peel zucchini. Stir-fry until slightly tender, for about five minutes. Do not overcook. Season with soy sauce that is not flavored or colored. This is an excellent way to prepare any vegetable. Serves 4.

### BAKED BANANAS

Plan on one banana per person. Place them whole and unpeeled on a baking sheet in a 350° oven. Bake for about 30 minutes. Peel bananas before serving them with lemon juice and brown sugar.

### SNACK

### PARTY MIX

Use one or more varieties of Chex. Combine with pretzel sticks that are not flavored or colored, instead of nuts. Melt 4 tablespoons butter in a baking pan and add the Chex and pretzel sticks, coating them well with the butter. Bake slowly in a 250° oven for 45 minutes.

---

### TUESDAY

| BREAKFAST | SCHOOL LUNCH | DINNER |
|---|---|---|
| Pineapple juice | Cheese sand- | Beef or lamb stew* |
| Eggs in toast | wich* | with vegetables |
| cups* | Corn chips | Herb dumplings* |
| Hot chocolate | (check label) | Pear and cream |
| | Banana | cheese (or cot- |
| | Milk | tage cheese) |
| | | salad* |
| | | French bread |
| | | Tapioca pudding |

## AFTERNOON SNACK

Cookies* and milk

### BREAKFAST

### EGGS IN TOAST CUPS

Slice bread and trim off crust (save in freezer). Grease muffin tins and press buttered bread slices into cups. Break an egg into each. Sprinkle with pepper and salt. Bake in a 350° oven for about 20 minutes, until eggs are set. If this requires too much time for a weekday, serve on Saturday.

### LUNCH

Cheese Sandwich—Use any Swiss or jack cheese, or any white cheese.

### DINNER

### BEEF OR LAMB STEW

Use cheaper cuts of meat. Brown well in oil or fat with 1 finely cut onion. Add water or stock and cook slowly for several hours. Add any vegetables in season (the more variety the better) during the last half-hour of cooking. Cabbage, broccoli and leaf vegetables need only 15 minutes.

*Note:* While stew is cooking, make syrup for breakfast on Wednesday. After dinner, prepare French bread for French toast. Both recipes are on Wednesday's list.

### HERB DUMPLINGS

Most of the biscuit mixes on the market contain no artificial flavoring or coloring, but check to make certain and then follow the recipe on the box for dumplings. Add chopped fresh or dried parsley for the herb flavor and color.

A word of caution: dumplings absorb a great amount of liquid in cooking. Be certain there is plenty of liquid in the pot or put in some more before adding the dumplings to the stew.

### PEAR AND CREAM CHEESE (OR COTTAGE CHEESE) SALAD

Use either canned or fresh pears. Thin mayonnaise with a little milk to use as dressing. Make small balls of the cream cheese and place one in the center of each pear. If cottage cheese is used, make balls with ice cream scoop.

### SNACK

There are a number of cookies on the market that do not have artificial flavor or color. However, it is less expensive to make them at home.

### JEA'S COOKIES

| | |
|---|---|
| 1 cup sweet butter or short-ening | ½ teaspoon soda |
| | 1 teaspoon baking powder |
| 1 cup white sugar | ¼ teaspoon salt |
| 1 cup brown sugar | 2 cups oatmeal |
| 1 teaspoon pure vanilla | 2 cups cornflakes (check |
| 2 eggs | label) |
| 2 cups sifted flour | |

Cream butter and add all other ingredients. Mix well. Drop from the end of a teaspoon onto a well-greased baking sheet. Bake in a 325° oven for 15 minutes. Yield: about 150 small cookies.

Sweet butter is suggested because other butter may be dyed. Crisco or other shortening may be substituted.

**WEDNESDAY**

BREAKFAST | SCHOOL LUNCH | DINNER
--- | --- | ---
Grapefruit seg- | Egg salad sand- | Pork roast*
  ments |   wich* | Vegetable casse-
French toast* | Potato chips |   role* with white-
Syrup* | Cookies |   Cheddar-cheese
Chocolate milk | Milk |   sauce*
 | | Green bean salad*
 | | Pineapple Upside-
 | |   Down Cake*

AFTERNOON SNACK

Bread, butter and sugar

**BREAKFAST**

FRENCH TOAST

Cut French bread from last night's dinner into slices about ¾ inch thick. Dip thoroughly in mixture of ¼ cup of milk to 1 egg and let stand in the refrigerator overnight. Brown in a skillet in 2 tablespoons butter; or the slices can be placed on a cookie sheet and browned under the broiler.

HOMEMADE SYRUP

Heat 1 cup of water to the boiling point, lower heat and add 2 cups of firmly packed Kleenraw or brown sugar. Stir until completely dissolved. If you have pure maple syrup available, you can add a little for extra flavor, but it is not necessary. Pour into a storage jar to keep in the refrigerator. Makes one pint to use on pancakes, waffles and French toast.

LUNCH

The hard-boiled eggs colored with beet juice can be used

for the egg salad. Check the wording on the chips bag carefully to see that no coloring or flavoring has been added.

### DINNER

Pork Roast—If a picnic cut is available, it is not only less expensive but very tasty. The rib end of a pork roast, while fatter than a loin, is not as dry when cooked. Lamb roast may be substituted for the pork.

#### FIONA'S VEGETABLE CASSEROLE

| | |
|---|---|
| 1 white turnip | 1 bunch leeks |
| 1 onion | 2 tablespoons shortening |
| 1 yellow rutabaga | 4 ounces chicken broth or |
| 2 carrots |     stock |
| 2 stalks celery | |

Dice all in small pieces. Cook in shortening until the vegetables are still crisp and not browned. Transfer to casserole with the chicken broth or stock. Cover and cook for 1 hour in 350° oven. Check to see that there is sufficient liquid while cooking. Serve with a White-Cheddar-Cheese Sauce. This casserole makes a fine luncheon dish when served with a fruit salad.

#### WHITE-CHEDDAR-CHEESE SAUCE

| | |
|---|---|
| 2 tablespoons butter | ¼ cup grated white Cheddar |
| 2 tablespoons flour |     cheese |
| ½ cup milk | ¼ teaspoon salt |
| ½ cup chicken broth | ⅛ teaspoon pepper |

Melt the butter in a saucepan. Add flour and cook until it bubbles. Add milk and chicken broth gradually and stir until thickened. Add the grated cheese. Season with salt and pepper.

189

Green Bean Salad—made with fresh, canned or frozen green beans. If fresh or frozen, cook first; then cover with French dressing and let stand in refrigerator until very cold. For canned beans, use the Blue Lake variety, if available, and drain well before the dressing is poured on.

PINEAPPLE UPSIDE-DOWN CAKE

| TOPPING: | BATTER FOR CAKE: |
|---|---|
| ¼ cup shortening | 4 eggs |
| 2 cups brown sugar | 1 cup sugar |
| 1 can sliced pineapple | 1 cup sifted flour |
| (halves can be used) | 1 teaspoon baking powder |

Melt shortening in an iron skillet. Spread evenly with brown sugar. Place half slices of pineapple on top of the sugar in a pattern, such as spokes of a wheel, with small pieces in the center. Make batter by mixing the ingredients listed. Pour a little of the batter into a well-greased custard cup or a small pan to make a cupcake for the next day's school lunch. Pour the rest of the batter over the fruit and bake at 350° until inserted toothpick comes out clean. Turn upside down before it cools.

Bread, Butter and Sugar—This old-fashioned snack after school is still delicious. Or use honey in place of sugar.

## THURSDAY

| BREAKFAST | SCHOOL LUNCH | DINNER |
|---|---|---|
| Sliced banana | Cold meat sand- | Corned beef hash |
| Cooked cereal* | wich* | casserole* |
| Chocolate milk* | Relishes | Zucchini pancakes* |
| | Cupcake | Fruit Salad* |
| | Milk | Chocolate cake* |

AFTERNOON SNACK

Lemon pops*

**BREAKFAST**

Cooked Cereal—Oatmeal or Cream of Wheat, or any other cooked cereal without flavoring or coloring. Check labels.
Chocolate Milk—prepared with homemade syrup.

**LUNCH**

Cold Meat Sandwich from the leftover pork, or any other cold meat. Luncheon meats *cannot* be used.

**DINNER**

CORNED BEEF HASH CASSEROLE

1 tablespoon shortening
1 medium-sized onion
3 boiled potatoes, cubed
1 can corned beef without
   flavoring or coloring,
   minced

Salt and pepper to taste
Approximately ½ cup half-
   and-half

Place shortening in frying pan and sauté the onion until soft. Add the potatoes, and the corned beef chopped into small pieces. Season. Put in a greased casserole. Pour over enough half-and-half to just moisten. Heat well.

Poached eggs can be served with the casserole on occasion. Most brands of corned beef are not colored or flavored, but it is difficult to find the prepared "hash" without the synthetics.

ZUCCHINI PANCAKES

4 small zucchini
2 whole eggs, slightly
   beaten

¼ cup flour
Salt and pepper to taste
Oil or shortening for cooking

Cut off ends of zucchini but do not peel. Grate coarsely. Add eggs and flour and mix well. Season with salt and pepper. Fry in a skillet with a small amount of oil or shortening, pancake size, until brown on both sides. Children usually like small pancakes.

### FRUIT SALAD

Use grapefruit, pears or pineapple; melon, if in season. All four fruits are salicylate-free. Use a thinned mayonnaise, or French, dressing, or none, if you prefer.

### CHOCOLATE CAKE

Use any favorite recipe with either Baker's Unsweetened Chocolate or Baker's German Sweet Chocolate. Here is one suggestion:

| | |
|---|---|
| 1 package German Sweet Chocolate | ½ teaspoon salt |
| 1½ cups sifted cake flour | ½ cup butter or shortening |
| 1 cup sugar | ¾ cup buttermilk |
| ½ teaspoon baking powder | 1 teaspoon pure vanilla |
| ½ teaspoon baking soda | 2 eggs |

Melt chocolate over low heat. Cool. Sift flour with sugar, baking powder, soda and salt. Stir butter or shortening to soften. Add flour mixture, half of the buttermilk, and the vanilla. Mix to dampen flour, then beat for 2 minutes in electric mixer at medium speed, or 380 vigorous strokes by hand. Add melted chocolate, eggs and the remaining buttermilk. Beat 1 minute longer, or 150 strokes. Bake in a 9-inch square pan which has been lined on bottom with paper, at 350° for 40 minutes or until cake tester comes out clean. Cool in pan for 15 minutes. Frost as desired.

# SAMPLE MENUS

## LEMON POPS

These can be made well in advance and kept in the freezer. Prepare lemonade from frozen mix. There are a number of products that are without artificial color and flavor. Usually they are well labeled. Pour lemonade in muffin tins or any small molds. Use butcher's skewers for sticks and freeze. They make fine iced suckers.

---

### FRIDAY

| BREAKFAST | SCHOOL LUNCH | DINNER |
|---|---|---|
| Mixed juice* (half pineapple and half grapefruit) | Tuna sandwich* | Quick Minestrone* |
| | Olives, carrots | Filet of sole with broccoli,* or |
| | Chocolate cake | any fish without tomatoes |
| Bacon and egg (nonflavored bacon) | Milk | Baked potato |
| Toast and milk | | Broiled grapefruit* |
| | | Cookies* |

#### AFTERNOON SNACK

White cheese with crackers

## BREAKFAST

Mixed Juice—Mix equal parts of canned pineapple and canned grapefruit juice. Premixed brands are likely to contain flavoring and coloring.

## LUNCH

Tuna Sandwich—Use homemade mayonnaise.

### DINNER

#### QUICK MINESTRONE

Cook a package of frozen mixed Italian vegetables according to directions on the package. Add a 46-ounce can of Swanson's Chicken Soup or 4 cups of homemade or other pure chicken broth. Heat well and serve with Parmesan cheese and French bread, or with Italian bread sticks.

#### FILET OF SOLE WITH BROCCOLI

| | |
|---|---|
| 1 lb. fresh broccoli or 1 pkg. frozen | 4 tablespoons butter |
| | 1 tablespoon flour |
| 8 small filets (if large, use only 4) | 1 lemon, juice only |

Cook fresh broccoli in boiling salted water for 5 minutes; divide into flowerets. If frozen, cook according to instructions on the package. Do not overcook. Wrap each filet of fish around a small portion of the broccoli, and roll up. Place on a baking sheet. (The rolls can be prepared well in advance and refrigerated until 30 minutes before serving.)

Melt the butter in a small saucepan, add the flour and lemon juice, stirring until thickened. If sauce should become separated by too much heat, a little cold water, added a teaspoonful at a time, will bring it back to the correct consistency. Put 2 tablespoons of the sauce over each fish filet and bake in 350° oven for 25 minutes. Serves 4.

#### BROILED GRAPEFRUIT

Sprinkle halved grapefruit with cinnamon and brown sugar and place in the oven on a baking sheet at the same time as the fish. Just before serving, put under the broiler for a minute.

GRETA'S EASY SUGAR COOKIES

½ lb. sweet butter
1⅓ cups sugar
2 eggs, yolks only

2 cups flour
fresh lemon juice or pure
   vanilla

Mix butter and sugar, add egg yolks and flour, then flavor. Make into two rolls and keep in refrigerator. Whenever needed, slice thinly and bake in 350° oven for about 15 minutes, until lightly browned.

---

## SATURDAY

| BREAKFAST | HOME LUNCH | DINNER |
|---|---|---|
| Melon or pine-apple | K-P Pizza* | Avocado and grapefruit salad* |
| Waffles* with homemade syrup | Red Cabbage Cole Slaw* | Baked ham |
| Chocolate milk | Lemonade | Baked squash cas-serole* |
| | | Lima beans |
| | | Frozen lemon custard* |

AFTERNOON SNACK

Helper's Choice Cookies

**BREAKFAST**

Waffles—You will find an easy recipe on a box of Fisher's Biskit Mix. Other brands, such as Bisquick, also are free of artificial colors and flavors, and provide many recipes that can be used for quick meals. The waffles should be served with homemade syrup.

**LUNCH**

K-P Pizza—This recipe is especially for children on the

K-P Diet but is an easy and satisfying substitute for other types of pizza, all of which contain tomato products.

Split English muffins in half. Spread well with Italian Pesto sauce, which can be purchased either frozen or canned in any Italian market or delicatessen. Pesto is made from basil leaves. Over this, place thin slices of white jack cheese or grated Swiss cheese or other white cheese. Sprinkle with oregano or mixed dry Italian spices and top with Parmesan cheese. Toast under broiler until cheese bubbles.

Ruth's Red Cabbage Cole Slaw—This salad has been a favorite of personnel in the Allergy Department of Kaiser-Permanente for twenty years, always served at Christmas parties.

Cut 1 head of red cabbage finely. Thoroughly drain 1 large can of crushed pineapple. Mix together with home-made mayonnaise to moisten. Do not thin mayonnaise because the pineapple will add sufficient liquid. Let stand in the refrigerator for ½ hour before serving. This blends the flavor and softens the cabbage.

**DINNER**

Avocado and Grapefruit Salad—Use a tart dressing or thin mayonnaise. Save grapefruit peel to make candy.

BAKED SQUASH CASSEROLE

| | |
|---|---|
| 1 medium squash or 1 frozen package | TOPPING: Crushed cornflakes or me- |
| 2 tablespoons sweet butter | ringue made of egg white |
| 2 tablespoons brown sugar | and sugar |
| Salt and pepper to taste | |
| Half-and-half or milk | |

Either steam or bake the squash, or use the frozen product. Mash with the butter and brown sugar. Salt and pepper to taste. Add half-and-half or a little milk until the right consistency. Put in greased casserole with a topping of finely crushed cornflakes (check labels for synthetics) or meringue. The cornflakes should be mixed with a little melted butter or shortening. The meringue can be made with egg whites left over from making Greta's cookies. Reheat in 350° oven.

### FROZEN LEMON CUSTARD ETHEL

| | |
|---|---|
| 3 egg yolks | Pinch of salt |
| ¾ cup sugar | 3 egg whites |
| ¼ cup lemon juice | 1 cup whipping cream |
| Rind of ½ lemon | |

Beat yolks, add sugar, lemon juice and rind, and salt. Cook in double boiler until thick. Cool. Add stiffly beaten whites, fold in whipped cream. Pour mixture into ice tray and freeze.

*Note:* If Saturday is bake day and you make a variety of cookies for the week, samples can serve as snacks. If you have a freezer, bake for the entire week and ice the cakes just before using.

Soak dried yellow peas for Sunday's lunch sometime Saturday evening.

---

### SUNDAY

| BREAKFAST | HOME LUNCH | DINNER |
|---|---|---|
| Papaya juice | Swedish pea | Chicken, Oriental |
| Omelette (plain, | soup* | style* |
| ham or white | German pan- | Mixed salad* |
| cheese) | cakes* | Brown rice* |
| Toast | Pineapple sauce | Vegetable in season |
| Chocolate milk | Milk | Cake with caramel |
| | | icing* |

## SNACK TIME

Celery, cheese, crackers

### BREAKFAST

As above, or serve juice with lunch for a combined brunch.

### LUNCH

SWEDISH PEA SOUP

| | |
|---|---|
| 1 lb. yellow peas | 1 onion, sliced |
| 3 quarts water | 1 bay leaf |
| 1 lb. slightly salted pork, diced | 5 peppercorns |
| | Pepper to taste |

Clean and soak peas in cold water overnight. Put in kettle with water and simmer for about 3 hours. During last hour of cooking, add pork cut into small pieces, a little sliced onion, bay leaf and peppercorns. A ham bone or pieces of ham will add flavor. Serve plain or with croutons from leftover crusts.

GERMAN PANCAKES

| | |
|---|---|
| 3 eggs | SAUCE: |
| ½ cup flour | 1 can crushed pineapple |
| 1 teaspoon salt | Cornstarch |
| ½ cup milk | |
| 2 teaspoons melted butter or other shortening | |

Beat eggs with a fork or wire whip until blended. Add flour and salt to eggs a little at a time, beating after each addition until smooth. Add milk ¼ cup at a time, again beating slightly. Add melted butter or shortening and mix. Have ready your largest frying pan, well greased on bottom and on sides as well.

Pour batter into frying pan and bake in a very hot (450°) oven for 10 to 15 minutes, until well puffed up and slightly brown. Reduce heat to 350° and bake for another 10 minutes. Have canned crushed pineapple slowly heating on the stove in a small saucepan. Thicken a little with cornstarch moistened with a little water. Serve the pancake with the sauce, lemon wedges and powdered sugar.

### DINNER
#### CHICKEN ORIENTAL STYLE

Marinate chicken, cut in pieces, in an unflavored soy sauce several hours. Sauté in butter or peanut oil until brown. Transfer to a baking pan and bake, covered, in a 350° oven for about 30 to 45 minutes. Remove cover and bake for another 15 minutes. Serve with any vegetable. Asparagus, when in season, can be fixed Chinese style to accompany this chicken. Asparagus should be thinly sliced on an angle before cooking. Cook as in Monday's recipe.

#### MIXED SALAD

Try a mixture of cooked vegetables with French dressing or mixed beans, including garbanzos. Or raw spinach, chopped, with lemon and oil.

#### BROWN RICE

Follow simple directions on package. See other recipes for rices.

#### E-Z DOES IT CAKE

¾ cup sugar
1½ cups sifted flour
¼ teaspoon salt
2 teaspoons baking powder

¼ cup melted shortening or oil
1 egg, beaten
¾ cup milk
1 teaspoon pure vanilla

Sift dry ingredients. Add the egg to the shortening, then add milk and vanilla. Combine with the dry ingredients. Stir and mix well. Pour into greased and floured shallow cake tin. Bake in 350° oven for about 20 minutes.

Aunt Han's Caramel Icing (Aunt Han is now ninety years old, but this is still the favorite recipe of all her nieces and grandnieces.)

| | |
|---|---|
| 1 pkg. light-brown sugar | ½ stick of butter |
| ½ pint coffee cream or half-and-half | 1 teaspoon pure vanilla |

Boil first three ingredients together until soft ball forms in a cup of cold water when tested. Remove from fire; add vanilla and beat with spoon until icing is thickened. Spread on cake at once.

# Suggested Meat Dishes

### LEG OF LAMB DE BUREN

Have your butcher remove the bone from a leg of lamb and butterfly the meat so that it will be flat in the broiling pan. Marinate the lamb for several hours in ¼ cup of olive oil, ⅛ cup white distilled vinegar and 1 tablespoon of mixed dry Italian seasoning. Place on broiling pan and broil on lowest rack for ½ hour with the flesh side up. Turn and continue broiling with skin side up for another 15 minutes. Baste once or twice with the marinade. To serve, slice down on an angle. Meat should not be dry, but slightly pink. Serves 6.

### SWEDISH CABBAGE ROLLS

This recipe comes from the home of a childhood friend and is a little different from most other cabbage rolls.

| | |
|---|---|
| 1 medium head cabbage | 1½ teaspoons salt |
| ¼ cup rice | ¼ teaspoon pepper |
| 1 cup water | 2 tablespoons butter |
| 1 cup milk | 1 tablespoon brown sugar |
| ½ lb. ground beef | ½ cup milk or cream |
| ¼ lb. ground pork | Flour |
| 1 egg | Salt and pepper to taste |

Place cabbage in boiling salted water, after cutting out core of cabbage from underside. Cook until leaves separate easily but are not too soft. Drain. Bring the cup of water to a boil, add rice and simmer until all water has evaporated.

Add milk and cook until rice is tender. Stir occasionally. After cooking, mix with the next five ingredients. Fill each cabbage leaf with some of the mixture. Roll and fasten with a toothpick.

Heat butter in a skillet. Brown cabbage rolls on all sides. Sprinkle with brown sugar and put in a casserole. Add juices from the skillet and a little water or stock. When serving, add the extra ½ cup of milk or cream and a little flour to juices in pan; correct seasoning with salt and pepper. Simmer until thickened. Should be cooked in a 350° oven for about 1 hour.

### TAMALE PIE

| | |
|---|---|
| 1 lb. ground beef | ½ cup sliced pitted ripe |
| 1 can cream style corn | olives |
| 1 envelope French's Taco | 1 pkg. Dromedary Corn- |
| Seasoning | bread Mix or any corn- |
| ½ cup water, brought to a | bread mix without syn- |
| boil | thetics |

Brown the beef lightly, add corn and French's Taco Seasoning, water and olives. Stir frequently. Keep mixture hot. Meanwhile, prepare cornbread batter. Pour the hot meat mixture into a shallow casserole and spoon the cornbread mixture on top. Bake in a 400° oven until topping is brown, about 15 minutes.

### TAMALE PIE VARIATION

This one is made with whole tamales. Be sure they contain no artificial flavoring or coloring. Break two tamales into small pieces and put in a greased casserole. Add 1 large can cream style corn, 1 can pitted ripe olives and ¼ lb. white Cheddar cheese, grated. Bake in a 350° oven for 30 minutes.

TACOS

Lightly brown ½ lb. ground beef. Stir in ½ pkg. French's Taco Seasoning or Lawry's Enchilada Sauce Mix with ½ cup water. Bring to a boil and simmer for 15 minutes. Spoon off extra fat. In filling taco shells heated in oven, add chopped onion, lettuce and white cheese slivers or Parmesan, grated, but omit any tomatoes.

PORK STEAKS

Have the butcher cut a fresh picnic cut of pork roast into 1-inch slices. Marinate in a mixture of 4 tablespoons unflavored soy sauce, mixed with 2 teaspoons sugar. Let stand for several hours. Bake in a 400° oven for ½ hour in the marinade.

VEAL SCALLOPINI VERA

2 tablespoons oil
1 stalk celery, sliced
1 sliced carrot
4 or 5 fresh mushrooms, sliced

2 or 3 slices veal, cut thin
Pinch of brown sugar
Oregano

Put 1 tablespoon of olive oil or other pure oil into a small saucepan and add vegetables. Cook until tender. If necessary, a little water can be added to the vegetables while they are cooking to keep them moist and to provide a good sauce. In a skillet, put the other tablespoon of oil, and over high heat brown very thin slices of veal, allowing 2 or 3 per person. When brown on both sides, add the cooked vegetables with a pinch of brown sugar and a sprinkle of oregano. Serve with noodles or spaghetti, with Pesto as a sauce for the pasta. This recipe is for 1 serving only.

### MARSH'S CHICKEN SHORTCAKE

1 pkg. Dromedary Corn-
   bread Mix, or any other
   cornbread mix free of
   additives
Sliced cooked ham
Leftover sliced chicken or
   turkey
Parmesan cheese

SUPREME SAUCE:
White sauce, made half with
   chicken broth and half
   with milk (homemade
   broth or Swanson's
   Chicken Broth or any
   other broth without artificial coloring or flavoring)

Bake cornbread according to directions on package. When cool, cut in pieces about 4 inches square, and then slice each piece in half through the center. Arrange on a baking sheet, one piece of cornbread for each serving. Over each piece of the bread, place a slice of ham and then a slice of chicken. Cover with Supreme Sauce and sprinkle with Parmesan cheese. Heat in a 350° oven for about 20 minutes, and just before serving, put under broiler for a few minutes to brown the cheese slightly.

# Suggested Side Dishes

### CORN PUDDING

6 eggs (2 eggs for each can of corn)
1 cup half-and-half
2 tablespoons sugar

Salt and pepper
½ cup melted shortening
3 cans white-kernel corn

Beat eggs, and add cream while beating. Add sugar and seasonings. Drain corn and put it in a greased baking dish. Pour butter (or whatever shortening is used) over corn, then egg mixture. Bake in a 350° oven until firm.

### BAKED NOODLES

1 pkg. medium noodles, cooked
1 cup cottage cheese
1 cup sour cream

1 finely chopped onion
Salt and pepper
Parmesan cheese

Mix all ingredients with the cooked noodles. Put in greased casserole and bake in a 350° oven until browned and crusty on top, about 40 minutes. Serve with extra sour cream and Parmesan cheese. In most cities there are locally made home-style noodles which do not contain synthetics.

### DAVID'S POTATO PANCAKES

4 large potatoes, grated coarsely
2 eggs

½ onion, finely grated
¼ cup flour
1 teaspoon salt

Add eggs to grated potatoes, add onions and stir until blended. Add flour and salt. Use large tablespoon to measure pancake and fry in skillet with any desired cooking fat or oil until brown on both sides. They can be made ahead of time and heated in short order. Serve plain or with sour cream. Small ones make wonderful appetizers (use a teaspoonful of mixture).

### HERMINE'S POTATO CUPS

4 large potatoes, grated
½ onion, finely grated
¼ cup fat or oil
2 eggs, slightly beaten

1 cup cornflakes, free of synthetics
¼ cup flour

Mix all ingredients well. Pour in well-greased muffin tins ¾ full and bake in a hot oven (400°) for 10 minutes, then turn oven down to 350° and bake for another 20 minutes. These are easy to serve. They will hold in the oven with the heat turned low, without losing any of their flavor. They become crisp when well browned.

### GREEN RICE

2 green onions
Garlic, if desired
½ cup olive oil
2 cups boiled rice

2 cups milk
2 cups grated white cheese
1 cup chopped parsley
2 eggs, slightly beaten

Chop onions and garlic. Cook in oil without browning. Add other ingredients. Bake in greased casserole for 45 minutes in a 350° oven. This dish will add natural color to the H-LD meal.

# Suggested Pickle Substitutes

### BELLE'S INSTANT MUSTARD BEAN PICKLES

1 cup sugar
½ cup white distilled vinegar
¼ teaspoon salt
8 teaspoons dry mustard

½ teaspoon minced onion
1 pkg. frozen wax beans, thawed, or 1 lb. can wax beans

Combine all ingredients except beans. Bring to boiling point, stirring until sugar and mustard are dissolved. Add beans and simmer, uncovered, for 5 minutes if frozen and thawed, 3 minutes if canned. Cool, cover and refrigerate. They will keep for several weeks.

### ROSE'S PICKLED ZUCCHINI

1 lb. zucchini
¼ lb. or 3 small onions, sliced
½ cup vinegar
½ teaspoon tumeric

2 teaspoons salt
½ cup sugar
½ teaspoon celery seed
½ teaspoon dry mustard

Scrub zucchini well, cut off both ends and slice thin. Do not pare off outer green. Cover with cold water and salt; soak for 1 hour. Mix all other ingredients and bring to a boil. Add zucchini, turn off flame, and let stand for 1 hour longer. Bring to a boil and cook for 3 minutes. Refrigerate.

# Suggested Cakes, Cookies and Sweets

### JOSH'S VANILLA WAFERS

1 cup sweet butter
1 cup sugar
2 eggs, well beaten

2 cups flour
2 teaspoons pure vanilla

Cream butter. Add sugar, then gradually eggs, flour and vanilla. Drop mixture from tip of spoon to a well greased cookie sheet. Bake in a 400° oven until edges brown. Watch closely; they take only about 10 minutes.

CY'S RICE PUDDING

| | |
|---|---|
| 3 eggs | ½ teaspoon pure vanilla |
| ½ cup sugar | 3 cups scalded milk |
| ¼ teaspoon salt | ¾ cup cooked rice |

Beat eggs slightly, add sugar, salt, vanilla and scalded milk. Put in buttered casserole. Add rice. Set in pan of water and bake in a 350° oven until knife in center comes out clean, from ¾ to 1 hour.

DOT'S SPONGE CAKE

| | |
|---|---|
| 5 egg yolks | 1 teaspoon pure vanilla |
| 1¼ cups sugar | 5 egg whites |
| 1¼ cups sifted cake flour | 1¼ level teaspoons cream |
| 5 tablespoons cold water | of tartar |

Beat yolks until light; add sugar gradually, continuing to beat. Add sifted flour and cold water alternately, then vanilla. Beat egg whites until foamy. Add cream of tartar and beat until stiff. Fold in egg whites and bake in an ungreased pan (one that has never been greased) in a 325° oven for 45 minutes. Test with a cake tester; if it is not completely dry, bake cake a little longer. Invert pan and cool. Then slide spatula around edge of cake, and it will drop out. Can be frosted, served plain, or dusted with powdered sugar. Save a few pieces to cut in the shape of ladyfingers to use the same week for cake below.

### FREDA'S ICE BOX CAKE

½ lb. Baker's German
  Sweet Chocolate
3 tablespoons sugar

3 tablespoons water
4 egg yolks
4 egg whites

Line cake form or individual ramekins or custard cups with pieces of sponge cake. Melt chocolate in a double boiler, add sugar, water and the egg yolks one at a time. Beat well after each addition. Cook slowly until thick and smooth. Cool. Add the stiffly beaten egg whites. Pour mixture into the cups or molds. Put in refrigerator for 12 hours or overnight. Add a tablespoon of pure whipped cream to each portion when serving.

### JOAN'S LEMON SQUARES

½ cup softened shortening
¼ cup confectioner's sugar
1 cup flour
1 cup granulated sugar
¼ teaspoon salt

½ teaspoon baking powder
2 eggs
Grated rind of ½ lemon
2 tablespoons lemon juice

Cream butter and sugar. Blend in flour, press evenly into bottom of 8-inch square pan. Bake for 20 minutes at 350°. Beat rest of ingredients together. Pour over baked crust and bake for 20 to 25 minutes longer. The filling puffs up during baking but flattens when cool. Cut into squares. Another yummy H-LD cookie.

### BANANA FRITTERS

1 cup sifted flour
¼ teaspoon salt
1 teaspoon sugar
1½ teaspoons baking powder

1 egg
¼ cup milk
2 bananas

Mix and sift together flour, salt, sugar and baking powder. Beat egg, add milk and stir into flour mixture, beating until smooth. Mash bananas and stir into batter. Fry in scant half inch of hot oil. Drain and sprinkle with powdered sugar. Serve as a dessert with hot homemade vanilla sauce or homemade chocolate sauce.

## Suggested H-LD Candies

### PAULA'S ENGLISH TOFFEE

¾ lb. sweet butter      I bar Baker's German Sweet
I lb. sugar      Chocolate, grated

Cook butter and sugar slowly in deep saucepan to the hard crack stage, 300° to 310°, until a ball pressed in a cup of cold water will be brittle and stay brittle when taken out of the water. A candy thermometer, of course, simplifies it all. Pour into a large buttered pan. Brush with the chocolate that has been grated. Put in refrigerator until hardened. Lift from pan and cover the other side with grated chocolate.

### BELLE'S CHOCOLATE FUDGE

2 cups white sugar      I cup half-and-half
2 teaspoons corn syrup      2 tablespoons sweet butter
2 squares Baker's Unsweet-      I teaspoon pure vanilla
    ened Chocolate      Pinch of salt

Put sugar, corn syrup, chocolate and half-and-half in a saucepan over low heat and stir occasionally. Boil until it forms a soft ball when dropped in a cup of cold water. It should hold together when rolled between the fingers. Add the butter, vanilla, and a pinch of salt. Let cool for about 10 minutes, if you can wait that long, and then beat well with a wooden spoon until thick and creamy. Pour into buttered pan and wait until cool to cut into squares. Beating is the only tiresome part, but you will have plenty of helpers to clean the pan and spoon. How we all loved fudge evenings!

THRIFTY CANDIED GRAPEFRUIT PEEL

2 grapefruit peels                    ½ cup water
1 cup sugar

Cut peel into narrow strips. These can be saved from breakfast for several days. Place peels in a small saucepan and cover with cold water. Let water come to a boil and drain. Repeat this 5 times to take away the bitter taste. Heat the sugar with the water, and when dissolved, add the peel. Cook slowly until the syrup is almost cooked away. With a fork, roll each strip in granulated sugar.


There are many other recipes which can be adapted for the K-P Diet. It is simply a matter of selecting the ingredients, using the diet list of "permitted" and "not permitted" items as a guide. Experimenting can be fun, and the H-LD child will thrive.

## About the Author

DR. BEN F. FEINGOLD taught pediatrics at Northwestern University Medical School in Chicago, following which he moved to Los Angeles, where for twenty-two years he practiced both pediatrics and allergy. He was chief of pediatrics at the Cedars of Lebanon Hospital, associate in allergy at the Los Angeles Children's Hospital, and attending pediatrician at the Los Angeles County Hospital.

In 1951 Dr. Feingold joined the Kaiser-Permanente Medical Care Program in Northern California as chief of the Department of Allergy. He was the founder and director of the Laboratory of Medical Entomology of the Kaiser Foundation Research Institute, and for twenty years chairman of Clinical Research for the Northern California Area of the Kaiser-Permanente Medical Care Program.

He is the author of numerous scientific publications and has lectured extensively to scientific as well as lay groups. His present studies in behavior in children serve as a basis for inquiries by committees of both the U.S. Senate and the state of California.